Praise for *The Forgot[ten Art of Love]*

"We know that love is a man[y splendored thing, but] what is this thing called love? *[The Forgotten Art of] Love* provides maps to greater understanding as well as ways better to appreciate some of the mysteries on the wide spectrum of what love is and what it isn't, along with insights on how to love. Armin Zadeh takes us beyond Eric Fromm's seminal *The Art of Loving* into a broader historical and contemporary understanding of what we really mean and may indeed be talking about when we talk about love."

— **Michael Krasny,** host of *Forum with Michael Krasny* and author of *Spiritual Envy*

"In *The Forgotten Art of Love* physician Armin Zadeh reminds us in eloquent and well-reasoned prose just how important and difficult healthy loving is. With a scientist's critical mind and an artist's careful eye, he unpacks the different types of love we all have the capacity to feel and in so doing teaches us how to feel them all. An inspiring book that couldn't be more timely!"

— **Alex Lickerman, MD,** author of *The Undefeated Mind*

"Wise, thoughtful, and beautifully written, *The Forgotten Art of Love* is a book you will not soon forget."

— **Daniel Gilbert, PhD,** professor, Harvard University, and author of *Stumbling on Happiness*

"If you're looking for a clearer understanding of the 'whys' behind love — as it applies to sex, religion, romance, society, and ourselves — take a deep dive into this enlightening philosophical and scientific exploration of all that love invites into our world. *The Forgotten Art of Love* guides you on a vast and fascinating mental trip in a space often reserved only for our hearts. Armin Zadeh is likely to change the way you think and feel about love in the process."

— **Scott Stabile,** author of
Big Love: The Power of Living with a Wide-Open Heart

"In a thought-provoking, accessible, wide-ranging, and ultimately satisfying analysis, Armin Zadeh addresses one of the greatest mysteries of life — what is love? Even more importantly, he describes how we can improve our capacity to love and how we can teach our children of its importance."

— **Peter Rabins, MD, MPH,** professor, Johns Hopkins
University, and author of *The Why of Things*

"Weaving together the insights from the ancient traditions and the latest neuroscience, *The Forgotten Art of Love* will inspire you to find the sublime beauty in everyday acts of love. This book will strengthen the many kinds of love that make our social lives so richly complex and meaningful."

— **Dacher Keltner,** professor of psychology,
UC Berkeley, and author of
The Power Paradox and *Born to Be Good*

THE FORGOTTEN
ART OF LOVE

THE FORGOTTEN
ART OF LOVE

What Love Means
and Why It Matters

ARMIN A. ZADEH, MD, PhD

New World Library
Novato, California

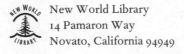 New World Library
14 Pamaron Way
Novato, California 94949

Text design by Tona Pearce Myers

Library of Congress Cataloging-in-Publication Data
Names: Zadeh, Armin A., author.
Title: The forgotten art of love : what love means and why it matters / Armin A. Zadeh.
Description: Novato, California : New World Library, [2017] | Includes bibliographical references and index.
Identifiers: LCCN 2017022096 (print) | LCCN 2017035513 (ebook) | ISBN 9781608684885 (Ebook) | ISBN 9781608684878 (alk. paper)
Subjects: LCSH: Love.
Classification: LCC BF575.L8 (ebook) | LCC BF575.L8 Z23 2017 (print) | DDC 177/.7—dc23
LC record available at https://lccn.loc.gov/2017022096

First printing, November 2017
ISBN 978-1-60868-487-8
Ebook ISBN 978-1-60868-488-5

Printed in Canada on 100% postconsumer-waste recycled paper

 New World Library is proud to be a Gold Certified Environmentally Responsible Publisher. Publisher certification awarded by Green Press Initiative. www.greenpressinitiative.org

10 9 8 7 6 5 4 3 2 1

Contents

Introduction

Love is a fundamental concern for all of us. Indeed, most people would list love as the most important element in a happy life. Yet our knowledge of how love evolves, how we can have love, and how it helps us attain happiness is surprisingly scant. For most aspects of life that are important to us, such as our hobbies or job, we typically spend many years training and mastering skills. People may spend weeks and months mastering a video game that may be of little relevance to the practicalities of life.

If love is so vital to us, why don't we invest similar effort to bring it into our lives and keep it strong? First, many believe that love is something we cannot control. We may think that we just have to be lucky, and love will come to us. I challenge this view and argue that anybody can find love. Another problem — particularly in the English language — is that the word *love* is not clearly defined: it has different meanings in different contexts. We may say, "I love ice cream," but we probably don't mean the same thing as when we say, "I love my children." We may also whisper, "I love you," to somebody on whom we have an enormous crush, but we may feel something quite different when we say the same to an old friend. Do we really mean *love* when we try to love our neighbors? Are these different loves? Is there a unifying concept of love?

I did not have answers to these questions thirty years ago, when a book on my parents' bookshelf grabbed my attention. Its title was *The Art of Loving,* by Erich Fromm, first published in the 1950s.[1] As a young adult, I hoped this was a new version of the *Kama Sutra,* and I eagerly pulled the book off the shelf. After overcoming my disappointment at finding a rather sober analysis of the phenomenon of love instead of practical instructions on lovemaking, I found myself drawn into the author's arguments. I read for hours in growing fascination.

Fromm described aspects of love that rang true to me but at the same time seemed contrary to the general perception of love. Fromm's concepts seemed helpful in addressing many problems in human relationships and the entire human condition. At the time, I did not know that I was holding an international bestseller that has helped thousands of people develop a fuller understanding of love. In a speech in London in December 1964, just days before he received the Nobel Peace Prize, Martin Luther

King Jr. hailed Fromm for identifying love as the "supreme unifying force of life."[2]

While I found Fromm's understanding of love compelling, I also felt that he did not get it entirely right. Several aspects of his descriptions and arguments struck me as incorrect, or at least incomplete. Furthermore, Fromm wrote his book in the context of the field of psychology in the 1950s, influenced by personal and widely prevalent religious views on the purpose of human existence. The book was written before the social revolution in the 1960s and before we gained vast insights into human biology in the late twentieth and early twenty-first centuries. I discussed Fromm extensively with my mother, a psychologist, and my father, a forensic psychiatrist, but I did not get satisfying answers to my questions.

In the 1980s, *The Art of Loving* was largely forgotten, read only by those with a keen interest in literature or psychology. Since that time, I have wanted to bring Fromm's ideas to a new generation, expanding his concepts and addressing their shortcomings. Love is a multifaceted phenomenon that affects many aspects of human life. Any attempt to view it solely from the angle of biology, psychology, sociology, spirituality, or philosophy will not do justice to its enormous complexity or its power over our lives.

Not being in the position to provide such a comprehensive view at that age, I parked my ideas on *The Art of Loving* in the back of my mind and continued with my education. I went on to study medicine and became a cardiologist, professor, and scientist. Even more important, I became a husband and a father. Naturally, these roles influenced my ideas about love. I continued my informal education on the subject, and these ideas continued to evolve over the decades; more, they became a steady companion in my activities.

As a physician, particularly one who takes care of patients with heart problems, one cannot afford to take too narrow a view of cardiac diseases when helping patients. Doctors need to understand how patients' emotions can affect their sensations and physical well-being. We know that heartfelt attention, the sense of physicians' and nurses' genuine care, has a tremendous influence on a patient's healing.

To understand a person's suffering, we need to understand the person. To understand the person, we must look at the human condition. What constitutes well-being and happiness? What makes a person hurt? The most severe physical pain may be easier to bear than emotional anguish. Among the worst forms of agony is a broken heart. Not only the end of a romance but the loss of any love can cause excruciating grief and misery. Love is the single most precious aspect of human life — even more precious than life itself. If we don't know about love, we don't know much about life.

In many ways, this book is the result of fifty years of living in search of answers about love. In the first twenty years, I was mostly passively absorbing ideas about love, particularly through the affection of my parents, family, and friends. The next thirty years involved active attempts to find answers to questions about love, many of them raised by Erich Fromm.

Going beyond Fromm's hypotheses, I explore love on the basis of contemporary insights into physiology and evolution. I attempt to disentangle love from commonly associated human instincts, such as sex and attachment, and discuss it in the context of society, philosophy, and religion. Last, I show the importance of educating our society, particularly our children, about love.

This book is not meant to be scholarly. Although I cite scientific articles to support some of my arguments and for further reading, this is not a literature review of scholarly research on love. Rather, I want to offer a framework for love that considers insights from different fields of human endeavors to formulate an understandable, constructive, and practical approach to love that is applicable to our daily lives. Our days can be filled with love. It is up to us to realize it.

1. What Is Love?

In our society, in songs, movies, and books, when someone feels an overwhelming sensation of longing for another person, we refer to it as *love*. This yearning may overtake everything else in a person's life and unleash previously undiscovered energy. It involves simultaneous feelings of ecstasy and agony because of our hopes for, and doubts about, the reciprocation of our feelings.

Being "in love" is one of the most exhilarating emotional states, and many people associate it with the greatest happiness in life. Most of us carry some kind of romantic love story with us, which may be based on novels, poetry, movies, or personal experience. The intensity of the feeling and its hold over our thoughts and actions are so extraordinary that we may remember it our whole lives. We may chuckle inside recalling the foolish things we did when madly in love and how anxious we were to get even the smallest shred of attention from the beloved one.

When we fall in love, the world seems different, and our heads spin with fantasies and dreams. It feels as if we are under a spell. Nothing matters except the beloved. The exhilaration mounts into ecstasy if the beloved person reciprocates our feelings. No wonder that most people yearn for this sensation and that its portrayal is so central to the arts and entertainment.

The most powerful stories in our culture center on love. Consider Paris and Helen in Greek mythology, Cleopatra and Mark Antony, Romeo and Juliet — the greatest poets and writers mesmerized readers with their love stories. But is it conceivable that Romeo's intense feelings for his Juliet were *not* love?

Erich Fromm radically challenged the idea that love consisted merely of intense feelings.[1] He differentiated *falling in love* from the *state of love*. He argued that the overwhelming sensations we experience when falling in love in fact are not love at all but a state of infatuation. This claim stirred up quite a controversy. But anybody who has ever been in love knows that the obsessive, all-consuming feelings of the early stages of a romantic relationship don't last. Eventually they fade, and while we still may feel very affectionate toward the beloved, we are not as infatuated as we were in the beginning.

Even couples still very much in love after decades admit that there is a distinct difference between the early and later stages of their relationship. Many marriages actually begin to crumble over the disillusionment that sets in when these very intense initial feelings begin to fade.

About half a century after Fromm, methods of biological analysis provided new insights into the phenomenon of romantic love. Researchers compared the blood levels of several hormones in individuals who had recently fallen in love with those in single people and people in long-term relationships.[2] They found higher levels of cortisol (a steroid hormone released in response to stress) and a number of other differences among blood hormones in the group that had recently fallen in love compared to those in long-term relationships. Furthermore, differences in hormone levels correlated with more intense feelings of falling in love, and hormone levels returned to normal in later phases of a relationship. The precise combination of hormones responsible for the emotions that arise when we fall in love has not yet been fully elucidated, but they include dopamine, oxytocin, glucocorticoids, endorphins, and amphetamines. These are hormones that may induce states of euphoria and, in the case of oxytocin, foster attachment. Indeed, the powerful effects of some of these hormones have been compared to those of cocaine.[3] Cortisol is also released when we are stressed, which explains why falling in love also has some uncomfortable effects, such as anxiety and sleeplessness.

New tools for studying the brain and nervous system have also yielded novel insights into love. Functional magnetic resonance imaging (fMRI) studies comparing the brains of two groups of people — those who had recently fallen in love and those in long-term relationships — corroborate the findings from blood-hormone analyses: they show some distinct differences in brain activity during these stages.[4] Specifically, the brain areas associated with compulsive behavior were much more active in people who had recently fallen in love than those in long-term relationships. These findings may explain our obsession with love during this phase.

Furthermore, studies show that the rise and fall of blood hormones associated with the falling-in-love phase are quite consistent and predictable. Typically, hormone levels return to the normal range after one to four years of courtship, and this decrease correlates with the fading of the intense feelings of being in love. Divorce rates peak at four years of marriage, suggesting that breakups may be linked to falling levels of love hormones and the associated decrease of powerful sensations.[5]

Blood analyses and brain MRIs thus suggest that falling in love is different from long-term love. While falling in love, we are totally consumed with thoughts of the beloved. Elevated levels of dopamine induce a state of euphoria and energy that is difficult to match even with the use of powerful drugs. Research has revealed that we fall in love instantly — within a second of looking at a person.[6] Subconsciously and at lightning speed, our brain runs through a list of criteria, and if these criteria are met, we fall in love. Because the list of criteria is extensive (and likely keeps expanding throughout our lives), we don't fall in love too often. Our criteria for falling in love are to some degree inherent, but they are also formed by our upbringing. If we pay close attention, we may recognize a pattern in the people we fall in love with.

Why do we fall in love? It appears to be nature's way of jump-starting a relationship. From the perspective of evolutionary psychology, the energy and euphoria generated in our brains serve to establish a strong bond between two people for the purpose of reproduction. Unlike the sex drive, however, falling in love functions not only to foster an environment for sexual intercourse but also to allow sufficient attachment between the partners that they will cooperate to protect the offspring beyond her or his most vulnerable period.[7] Three to four years of coupling is generally sufficient time for successful childbearing and for guarding children through the stage of entire helplessness. After that, one parent is often able to safely raise the offspring to reproductive age — the critical goal for evolution. Since evolution is all about efficiency, falling in love only needs to last about three to four years.

This is a sobering view. Are all of these wonderful feelings just nature's way of inducing us to mate and reproduce successfully? Is love programmed not to last? Well, the answer depends on whether we equate the sensations experienced when we fall in love with those we experience when we *love*. To address these issues, we need to define love — which is not an easy task. For millennia, philosophers, spiritual leaders, poets, writers, and others have tried to define love, but we still have no widely accepted definition that takes into account all its complexities.

Some philosophical texts contend that love cannot be defined at all.

Interpretations and definitions of love are strongly influenced by societal, philosophical, and spiritual beliefs. Thus, love may have different meanings in different cultures. And many of the feelings frequently associated with love are, in my view, not part of the spectrum of love itself.

Gottfried Leibniz, a German polymath and philosopher in the seventeenth century, defined love as the capacity "to be delighted by the happiness of others," which captures much of the essence of love.[8] If we love somebody, we indeed derive a sense of bliss from seeing them happy. Most of us have known the contentment that comes from seeing the joy in our loved one's eyes. On the other hand, Leibniz's definition of love does not take into account the intensity of the lover's emotion or his/her active role in creating it. "Being delighted by the happiness of others" can describe both a fleeting moment of sympathy and the lasting, deep sensation of love.

A more precise definition of love might be *the urge and continuous effort for the happiness and well-being of somebody (or something)*. Thus, love is a more intense form of caring or compassion. Love is associated with a stronger impulse, greater satisfaction, and more intense emotion than simply caring. But the border between compassion and love is not sharply delineated. It is a matter of degree — of the intensity of our feelings and our level of commitment, such as our willingness to make sacrifices for someone else's well-being. For example, we may chat with a neighbor once in a while. We like her, and when we hear that she has broken her hip and needs help with commuting or grocery shopping, we gladly offer to help. However, we would not quit our job or make some other big sacrifice in order to help her. These are things we would do for people we love, those to whom we are very close. Thus, our commitment to the well-being of others and our associated emotions determine whether we consider it love or merely compassion.

Just as we find it difficult to define love, we have no comprehensive understanding of how love originates. Contrary to the common view that love descends upon us without any conscious volition on our part, Fromm argued that love is an *activity*, something that requires enormous effort and concentration — in fact, an art. To master the art of loving, we must devote ourselves to it and give it priority over all other activities. Fromm argued that we can essentially love anybody if we commit ourselves to the effort. Loving is not a matter of the object of our love, but of the subject, meaning our own perception of someone we love.

Fromm's view of love was enthusiastically embraced by many but also met with criticism. Some people felt that such a sober, rational description left out the emotional aspects of love and ruled out the possibility of a unique bond between two people. Indeed, emotions are essential to loving. Everybody recognizes the sensation of delight in looking at a loved one and feeling the urge to hug and hold that person. These feelings persist after the falling-in-love phase: they are an intrinsic part of love. While Fromm was right to emphasize the active, conscious component of love, I believe he shifted the balance too far and created an overly cerebral, intellectual concept of love.

Love has both active and passive components. Active loving involves the conscious or subconscious prioritizing of loving over other human impulses. The emotions of loving, such as joy at seeing the happiness of the beloved, on the other hand, come naturally — that is, they are passive. These emotions are the spontaneous *result* of the act of loving. If we reflect on the most blissful emotions we have ever felt, we are likely to recall the joy of seeing the elation of a child or partner. This is the greatest reward for loving, filling our hearts with warmth and the utmost contentment. But to experience these ecstatic feelings, we must first have actively triggered the process of loving in our minds (consciously or subconsciously).

Unlike the emotions that accompany falling in love, the feelings we experience as a part of love will persist as long as we continue to work at loving. Actual love typically demands knowledge of the beloved — much more than we need to know in order to fall in love with somebody. Often, instant passion can be triggered merely by physical features or a brief encounter. This passion allows us to develop an idea of the beloved person that is largely based on our own hopes and desires and may not reflect reality. I recall the first time being "madly in love" when

I was sixteen and spotted a girl in a dance club. I did not have the courage to talk to her but, mesmerized by her appearance, I drove twenty miles on my moped through rain and snow every day for weeks back to that same dance club in the hopes she would return — without ever having spoken a word with her. Thus, we may well fall in love with our *perception* of a person. As we spend more time with the object of our passion, that perception may conflict with the person's actual nature — which sometimes may lead to disappointment or disillusionment. The state of exhilaration, however, may mask the disappointment for some time (leading to denial). If two people have no adequate understanding of love at this point, their relationship stands little chance of surviving.

Many people resist the notion that the intense feelings that accompany falling in love can be dismissed as mere infatuation. Some also reject the distinction between infatuation and love as purely academic and inconsequential. But this distinction actually matters tremendously for our lives. The falling-in-love phase invariably ends. If we interpret the fading of these intense feelings as the end of love itself, we may question the whole basis of our relationship. Couples are often distraught when they realize they are not as crazy about each other as they were in the beginning. Instead of acknowledging the ephemeral nature of falling in love, they often break up to look for a new rush in another partnership — only to repeat the cycle. Partners who expect to remain in a state of euphoria forever will inevitably be disappointed.

The ensuing disappointment not only causes heart-ache for the couple but often has devastating consequences for the people around them, especially children. The cliché of "lovesick fools" holds some truth: when our minds are flooded with the hormones of falling in love, our judgment can be impaired. MRI studies of the human brain have consistently shown that brain areas responsible for decision making are greatly influenced by the emotions that accompany falling in love.[9] When the infatuation phase of courtship ends, lives may be thrown into disarray.

My friend Ben met his wife, Sandra, at work right after college. Ben fell in love with Sandra almost instantly in the office hallway. He had barely spoken with her, but he was captivated by her looks and her vivacious, funny style. His obsession with her grew, and soon he found himself fantasizing about her most of the time. When he ran into her in the office, his heart pounded, and he froze. He desperately wanted to ask her out on a date, but he felt so awkward in her presence that he could not do it.

It was Sandra who took the initiative. She had noticed Ben, too, and was attracted to him. They went for a drink after work and found themselves talking for hours. Everything felt right, and they felt as if they had known each other forever. They became inseparable. After three months of dating, they moved in together. After another eight months, Ben asked Sandra to marry him. Sandra got pregnant in the second year after their wedding and again one year later.

In the beginning, everything seemed perfect, and they never quarreled. Over time, however, tensions began to rise. Rather than go back to work, Sandra wanted to stay at home with the children. Struggling to earn enough money to support the family, Ben took on a second job and felt increasingly tired. When he came home, he wanted to do nothing but eat and watch television. It seemed to him that Sandra did nothing all day except play with the kids, while he was working himself into the ground. When he wanted to spend more time with his friends and Sandra objected to his going out without her, he became resentful.

Sandra was irritated by Ben's messiness and his unwillingness to help out at home. She had noticed early in their relationship that Ben was untidy, but at first she was only mildly amused, and she always cleaned up after him. Gradually she grew angry and resentful when he left things in disarray, feeling overwhelmed with housework and childcare and upset at not getting any appreciation from Ben.

The incredible attraction they had felt for each other faded away. Ben felt drawn to other women at work, and Sandra fantasized about one of her friends from college. They fought almost daily, usually about trivial things. They grew further and further apart, and six years after their wedding they consensually filed for divorce.

What happened? How could the intense feelings they had felt for each other disappear? When they met, they had no doubt they were made for each other. Both had been sure that what they perceived as true love would last forever.

In truth, Ben and Sandra never loved each other — at least not in the sense that I use the term *love*. They fell in love but never made the transition to true, mature love. Ben and Sandra enjoyed their blissful emotions but failed to make the continuous effort that love requires. In other words, neither of them put the other's happiness and well-being above everything else. When their infatuation-boosted hormones ebbed, they did not work at fostering love. Eventually, the realities of life caught up with them.

Job and family place high demands on us. It is difficult to pick up after ourselves and help out around the house when we are tired out after a long day of work. It may be hard to welcome a partner with a smile after the children have driven us to the brink of insanity all day. Our first reaction to expectations of this kind is to feel frustrated and irritable. Only when we push these impulses aside and focus on our love for our partner and family can we learn to feel happy despite these pressures.

Focusing on love gives us the energy and motivation to do the things we may perceive as contrary to our immediate interests. The desire to see our loved ones happy can encourage us to do whatever we can to make their lives better. But this love has to be constantly rescued from being overshadowed by other, more self-serving urges. It requires us to be continuously mindful of our true priorities. This is a great challenge.

For most of us, the ability to love has to be learned and practiced. Sandra and Ben gave up on their relationship before they really got started. Once the excitement was gone, they thought their love was over: they never gave themselves the opportunity to experience true love. In their state of infatuation, they not only rushed into a marriage, but they also had children, who are now facing an upbringing by parents who live apart and are in conflict over custody issues, legal expenses, and other problems.

How would understanding the distinction between falling in love and actual love have made a difference to Ben and Sandra? Knowing that people often don't think rationally while falling in love, Ben and Sandra could have enjoyed their mutual infatuation with just enough perspective to wait a little before getting married. Once the butterflies were gone, they might have assessed the situation more soberly. At that point, they might have either consciously taken the next steps to develop a mature love or separated before making a long-term commitment. One of the most common reasons given for divorce in the United States is "unrealistic expectations."[10] A mature view of love would have given Ben and Sandra the wisdom to know what is required for maintaining a partnership and to recognize whether they were ready for it.

Western society does a lot to mislead us about the concept of love. Every day we are deluged with images of love as magical, serendipitous, and exhilarating. Almost invariably, romantic movies tell the story of a couple falling madly in love, usually after some cute or harrowing plot twists that lead them into each other's arms. The story inevitably ends with a proposal of marriage and the prospect of living happily ever after.

Most fictional love stories describe two people falling in love but typically do not describe their lives a few years later. It is easier to portray that exhilarating state of being drunk with love than the period when the hormone levels decline. However, when our popular images of love focus on falling in love while neglecting the arguably more important task of maintaining love, we often get the wrong idea about love altogether.

The entertainment industry, of course, keeps making these stories because they are tremendously popular. Who doesn't want to find love the way people do in the movies? Like Cinderella, we want our perfect lover to appear magically at our door. Likewise, we enjoy stories of people who become rich overnight because of a lucky twist of fate — because we imagine that someday it might happen to us. A story of success achieved through hard labor, discipline, and determination may be inspiring, but it is much less exciting, let alone romantic. In the age of internet billionaires, the entertainment industry's concept of love fits perfectly. Unfortunately, Hollywood's take on love is just as unrealistic as most of its other creations. While any of us may indeed fall madly in love at any moment, it requires effort and dedication to keep the fire alive.

Is it true that we all have one perfect partner somewhere out there in the world? Undoubtedly there are couples whose personalities are exceptionally compatible.

But the human personality is so complex that complete agreement on any aspect of life is exceedingly unlikely. There is almost always room for improvement in a relationship. Even so, many of us remain sentimentally attached to the idea of this one true love, whose unwavering devotion will survive parting and even death. While there is nothing wrong with this belief, people who adopt it may make life harder on themselves by turning their backs on other possibilities. Each of us is unique, and we may love the unique beauty in more than one person.

As a cardiologist, I find this difficult to admit, but love is more about the brain than the heart. We may savor the elements of chance, magic, and fate in romance and love. Subconsciously, we also want to believe in the role of fate because it lets us deflect responsibility for the lack of love in our lives. It may be easier to believe that we are unlucky in love than to acknowledge that we have not devoted ourselves sufficiently to finding and nurturing love. And the idea that love may strike at any moment is also a source of enduring hope. A concept of love based on effort and focus — without any stroke of magic in its emergence — may not be good news to those who rely on serendipity.

However, the sober view of love as a mental rather than a magical power comes with a silver — if not golden — lining. Embracing our ability to create love is empowering: it means we can fill every moment of our lives with love. We don't have to wait for the magic of love to strike: we can have it all the time. No, we cannot manufacture or control the intensely euphoric feelings of falling in love, but they are fleeting anyway. The lasting, satisfying contentment from love is ours for the making.

No matter what its source, experiencing love is beautiful. Nothing moves the human soul like love. Goethe's Faust spends decades studying philosophy, medicine, theology, and more, only to find that it is love that truly moves him to excitement. The mere fact that strangers meet and form unbreakable bonds for life is nothing short of miraculous. Love can unleash determination and forces we never knew existed within us. Knowing that love is indeed an art that we can foster and advance should only increase our excitement about love.

We do not have to be sad about the transient nature of falling in love. On the contrary, knowing that it is fleeting can allow us to embrace it even more closely and cherish every moment. Knowing its physiological causes and its transience may give us the necessary perspective to prevent ourselves from making poor decisions during this time. We may intentionally postpone considerations about marriage and children until after three to four years of courtship to be sure that our relationship has a good chance of lasting.

Knowing that we cannot take ourselves too seriously while we are falling in love may also reduce the anxieties of this state. We can laugh a little at ourselves and indulge in the sweetness of the feeling without fully succumbing to it. We can recognize that our infatuation when we are falling in love may be a wonderful introduction to a relationship, as long as we are willing to play an increasingly active part in moving to the lasting, and even more rewarding, state of love.

Typically, we continue to feel very strong emotions and affections for a partner after the falling-in-love phase. Couples who are committed to their relationship often find that infatuation develops into love. The fact that our experience of love is largely under our control opens the door for happiness and opportunities. We don't have to wait and see if we are lucky enough to find love: we can have it as soon as we make loving a priority in our lives. It would be nice if love indeed simply presented itself to us and stayed forever without much effort on our part. However, love is no exception to another fundamental rule in life: nothing comes from nothing. Most things of value in life need to be earned; they are the reward for devotion and effort. The reward for working at loving can be immense.

2. Why Do We Love?

Let us now go deeper into the subject and explore the essence of love. What is the nature of loving? Why are humans so preoccupied with love? What makes us love a particular person? These questions have been asked throughout human existence. Religious thinkers, secular philosophers, artists, and scientists have answered them in different ways.

Contemplations about love and its significance can be found as early as three thousand years ago in the teachings of Zarathustra, the ancient Iranian prophet. Considered by many to be the first philosopher, Zarathustra taught that by doing good to others, we align ourselves with the divine force and move closer to being one with the creator.[1] He captured essential themes of love that have been reiterated by many prominent thinkers since.

Even ancient contemplations of love differentiate between the forms I have already discussed: a physically driven desire for human contact, close to what we would categorize as lust, described in Hinduism and Buddhism as *kama;* a less intense form of caring that we would call compassion, known in Buddhism as *karuna;* and the highest, most noble, and elevated form of love, which is unconditional and selfless — described in Hinduism as *prema* and in Buddhism as *metta,* with equivalents in other religious texts.

Similar distinctions can be found in the best-known comprehensive discussion on the nature of love, in Plato's *Symposium,* from approximately 380 BCE.[2] Plato discusses different analyses of love by assuming the identities of contemporary intellectuals. In the discussion, the character Pausanias describes two kinds of love: a *heavenly* love — a deep love associated with the intellect that is long-lasting and committed — and a *common* love, driven by physical attraction and lust. Thinkers more than two thousand years ago recognized the complexity of love, its multifaceted nature, and the difference between short-term infatuation and lasting love. Plato makes a clear distinction between affection based on sexual desire, fleeting passion, and a deep, enduring concern for another person (true love).

In the same text, Plato's teacher, Socrates, portrays love as the force striving for divinity, arguing that our fear of death and our yearning for immortality are expressed in our physical and intellectual desire for procreation. *Platonic love* is a term commonly used today to refer to nonsexual love, but it is more accurately defined as the yearning for the unattainable, ideal beauty in the world that may be reflected in somebody or something. The recognition of this beauty or purity in a person moves us closer to divinity. In Plato's conception, we feel love not for the individual but rather for the inherent beauty in that person, a beauty that transcends individual existence. Thus, a person who loves one person in fact loves the beauty in *any* person — a very astute and important observation. Plato went beyond descriptions of a selfless, caring attitude toward others and attempted to understand its underlying cause.

For many centuries, Plato's concepts of love, which his students, particularly Aristotle, expanded on, profoundly influenced views of love. Indeed, the ancient Greek terms are still being used for describing different kinds of love, as in C. S. Lewis's 1960 book *The Four Loves*.[3] *Philia* refers to brotherly love, or loving friendship. *Storge* is generally understood as the somewhat more intense bonds between parents and children or exceptionally close friends. *Eros* refers to the passionate and romantic feelings, closest to falling in love. Finally, *agape* refers to the highest form of love, a transcending, unconditional love, particularly the love between humans and God. This rich Greek vocabulary suggests that much of the confusion over the meaning of love arises from the fact that in English we have only one word to describe a wide range of emotional states and concepts.

The emergence of Islam in the seventh century CE gave rise to the concept of *ishq*, or divine love. In the Sufi tradition of Islam, love is essential to lead humans back to our destiny of grace.

The Middle Ages in Europe engendered the tradition of *courtly* love that prized chivalry and nobility over erotic desires. This form of love, too, was believed to elevate the lover and the beloved to a higher level of being. While the concept of courtly love was influenced by religion, it was a secular concept, contrasting with the views of thinkers of that period such as Thomas Aquinas, who based his reasoning about love solely on Christian dogma. Given that courtly love centered on chivalry and male valor, it also neglected the role of women in mutually loving relationships.

In the seventeenth century, Baruch Spinoza proposed a concept of love that is linked more to nature than to the conventional concept of God.[4] Spinoza saw God not as a person but as an all-encompassing entity, one that includes nature. To him, love was one of the natural phenomena, "passions," which humans pursued because of their associated rewards, in this case joy. Spinoza's views are among the earliest recognitions of love as a physiological drive. At a time when discussions on love and God were dominated by biblical views, Spinoza's rational analyses of love and God earned him much criticism from the major established religions.

The nineteenth century saw a definite turn to biology and science for explaining love. Arthur Schopenhauer was the first prominent thinker to emphasize the biological aspect of love and its significance for human existence.[5]

Before Charles Darwin formulated his theories of evolution, Schopenhauer was already asserting that love is a powerful biological force essential to the success and survival of the human species. With his "will to live" paradigm, Schopenhauer identified love as a basic instinct with the purpose of facilitating reproduction. These concepts introduced biology as an important underlying mechanism for humans' feelings and expression of love.

Charles Darwin is best known for formulating the scientific theory of evolution. In this context, his paradigm of the "survival of the fittest" has often been interpreted to mean the "survival of the strongest and most powerful." In recent years, scientists have taken a closer look at Darwin's later work, which deals specifically with *human* evolution. In his book *The Descent of Man*, Darwin argued that morality and conscience are the most important factors in human evolution.[6] He concluded that empathy and other social instincts are rooted in biology, generating the basis of morality. Love and morality provide a survival advantage for our species by fostering and strengthening bonds between humans, leading to better protection of their offspring. Darwin acknowledged that he overstated the effect of the egotistic human drive in his earlier work, whereas in fact both selfish and altruistic instincts are in play in the process of evolution.

The twentieth century witnessed the fusion of evolutionary concepts of love with an emphasis on psychology, early childhood development, and sexuality, particularly among Sigmund Freud and his followers.[7] Freud saw love predominantly as an expression of the sexual drive, a view that was consistent with the paradigm of reproduction as the underlying force in love. Psychology dominated the thinking on love for decades to come, exploring the motivations for love and romantic relationships.

In the 1950s, Erich Fromm drew a categorical distinction between falling in love and actual love (see chapter 1). He viewed love as a deliberate construct of the mind, one that requires effort and focus: that is, an art. He theorized that love is a response to humans' innermost fear, that of loneliness. By facilitating union between people, love provides the remedy to our anxiety about human separation and awareness of our mortality. Fromm's theory of love is based on both psychological theory and religion.

In his 1973 book *Colours of Love*, John A. Lee expands on categories of love formulated by the ancient Greeks: *eros* (passionate love), *ludus* (game-playing love), *storge* (friendship), *pragma* (practical love), *mania* (possessive, dependent love), and *agape* (altruistic love).[8] The psychologist Robert Sternberg proposed a "triangle theory of love," consisting of intimacy, passion, and commitment.[9] Lee and Sternberg, however, describe patterns and components of relationships but not love itself. Love may be an important element in relationships, but other factors influence the dynamics of interpersonal bonds.

All these discussions of love through the centuries agree on some basic points. We refer to love in a number of ways: as an intense longing for another person that is associated with a highly euphoric state and a strong drive for connection and intimacy; as a passionate desire for physical closeness and sexual activity; and as a selfless concern for the contentment of others that may vary in intensity, ranging from benevolence toward neighbors and friends to, in its highest form, a feeling of mystical or spiritual union, that is, love of God or the divine. Over time, we have come to give more weight to the biological and psychological explanations of love than to religious theories.

Today, we can also bring the tools of neuroscience and endocrinology to bear on questions about how we perceive and experience love. Given the extreme complexity of the human brain and nervous system, we are only now starting to understand how our emotions, thoughts, and perceptions are directly related to the integrity, performance, and coordination of our nervous system. With modern brain imaging techniques, many thought processes can be located in specific areas in the brain. Functional magnetic resonance imaging techniques can now identify areas of the brain that are associated with different emotional states.[10] For example, we know which brain areas control fear, anxiety, and sadness, and we can modulate these responses using pharmaceuticals.

In recent decades, biomedical scientists have begun studying emotions that we commonly associate with romantic relationships, such as attraction, passion, and attachment. We know that an array of hormones influence mating and partnership behavior.[11] Studies demonstrate that different brain areas are active during early phases in a romantic partnership, such as the falling-in-love phase, than in long-term relationships.[12] Furthermore, these studies have found that distinct areas of the brain are active when people experience feelings of lust and attachment, indicating that these are different phenomena.[13]

It is now generally accepted that human behavior is largely motivated by basic instincts or drives. When we feel hungry, we are motivated to find food. When we are tired, we want to sleep. These brain imaging and hormone studies support the idea that sexual arousal, attachment, and love are distinct human drives.

Human drives evolved through natural selection over millions of years and serve the same purpose for all life: fostering the survival of the individual and the species. The evolutionary advantage of the human sex drive is easy to understand: it directly supports reproduction by allowing the combination of two people's DNA to create progeny. The intense, obsessive focus on somebody with whom we fall in love promotes mating, as well as partnership for the most vulnerable period of the offspring's life. Our egotistic impulses also make sense from an evolutionary perspective, as they promote our own well-being in order to allow procreation and to protect our children. By the same token, pronounced egotism, manifested in a strong drive for status and power, is still prevalent today because in the past it extended an advantage to individuals of high standing in a community, who could provide more resources and protection to their offspring. Consistent with Darwin's theories, recent research on evolutionary history has revealed that the association of social status and reproductive success weakened with human development and socialization.[14] At the same time, empathy and love have become more powerful forces for human expansion.[15]

Is love as I define it here — *the urge and continuous effort for another person's happiness and well-being* — also an evolutionary drive? A strong argument can be made that it is. Human brain imaging studies suggest that love is associated with numerous brain activities and tightly woven into our neural reward system.[16] Loving somebody activates brain areas that stimulate the production of hormones eliciting pleasant sensations and contentment. Love facilitates commitment in partnerships and provides a supporting structure for procreation. Love for our children is critical in nurturing them to reproductive age and providing them with the knowledge necessary for survival. Not surprisingly, love for our children is deeply rooted in us and is often described as the easiest, most naturally occurring love.

In addition, love fosters relationships and communities within our species and has likely been instrumental in the proliferation of the human race.[17] By forming large groups, humans have been able to defend themselves against predators and hostile environmental conditions, locate and secure food sources, and support one another in times of illness or injury. Within these groups, love has been instrumental to peaceful cohabitation and a comforting force for people enduring sickness, wars, and other hardships. At the same time, peaceful cohabitation has allowed different populations to exchange knowledge, which has led to advancements in crafts, sciences, and medicine.

Instincts and drives ultimately serve the purpose of promoting the species' survival. Some do so by supporting the individual, such as hunger, thirst, and aggression; others, such as the sex drive, work directly to foster population growth without promoting the individual's survival. In contrast, love supports the human species' survival by directly serving both the population *and* the individual. People with loving characteristics find it easier to build relationships and social alliances that provide protection for themselves and their progeny. Living in loving relationships is associated with better health and survival.[18]

The impulse for love seems to stand in opposition to other evolutionary human drives, such as aggression, egotism, and pursuit of power, which are directed toward self-preservation. In other words, love, despite conveying some benefits to the individual, appears to be largely aimed at directly preserving the species. The drive of love competes with and may even supersede the instinct of self-preservation. Consider a person whose family is caught in a burning house. The person is well aware of the risk of perishing in the flames, but many, if not most, of us would still try to enter the house to rescue our loved ones. We all know stories of people drowning or freezing to death while trying to save other people. From an evolutionary point of view, the fact that love trumps survival in these incidents is intuitive, because the drive for preserving the species (represented by fellow humans in danger) should be stronger than the survival impulse of the individual, if both are at risk. When people risk their lives to save others, we consider them heroes, not fools. Our intuitive admiration for self-sacrificing people may indicate that certain structures in our brain are wired to reward such acts, ultimately prioritizing the species over the individual.

From the standpoint of evolutionary biology, then, we might conclude that love is merely one of many human impulses geared to preserve the human species. This view is supported by evidence from research in other primates that show behavior similar to that of humans in loving relationships.[19] But why does love feel so important to us? Why is it among the first things anybody wishes for? Why does it even trump our desire for power, which provides a strong, proven evolutionary advantage?

The answer, again, may be quite sobering and mundane: the impulse for love is associated with more lasting and more pleasant feedback from the reward centers in the brain than other impulses are. A burst of aggression and the associated surges of adrenaline may cause brief feelings of empowerment and strength, but after these fleeting sensations subside, we typically feel empty and even remorseful. Many common activities, such as eating and sex, are associated with the blood hormones that induce euphoric feelings, but their effect is transient also. We tend to engage in these activities repeatedly to gain recurrent satisfaction, but they will never provide sustained contentment. On the contrary, allowing our self-serving impulses to prevail may cause dissatisfaction because they preoccupy our mind until they are satisfied. Particularly in Buddhism, desire is identified as the root cause of human suffering and dissatisfaction. Even the fulfillment that derives from powerful social status does not grant lasting satisfaction, as it typically comes with a desire for even greater standing and fear of loss of status. Conversely, allowing love to prevail and to steer our actions is associated with feelings of deep, sustained contentment and satisfaction, the sensations connected with lasting happiness.

Through natural selection, our brain has developed a system for rewarding certain impulses that support the individual's survival. These typically result in short-term pleasure and gratification. It appears, however, that the satisfaction from controlling self-serving instincts and responding to our drive to love supersedes that of all other impulses — not necessarily providing maximum euphoria but leading to lasting contentment. Once again, this outcome is logical from an evolutionary perspective, as love promotes both the survival of the individual *and* that of the species.

An impulse that preserves the individual is important, but it is overtaken by a drive that is even more critical for the survival of the species. Thus, the drive to love receives the greatest reward from our brain. Rewarding the process of rejecting self-serving impulses (rather than allowing them to prevail for short-term satisfaction) results in sensations of contentment.

In practice, both self-serving and altruistic impulses are instrumental in fostering the species' survival. The key concept of life is balance. An individual who ignores instincts for self-preservation is likely to perish prematurely; on the other hand, someone who behaves unlovingly risks social isolation (and lack of protection). Given the reward system of our brain, we are most closely aligned with our biology — receiving reinforcement for our behavior through sensations of contentment — if we focus our thoughts and actions on love while conceding to other impulses only as far as is necessary to sustain ourselves. Philosophical and spiritual conceptions of love as the vehicle that helps us achieve our *destiny* or *natural state of grace* follow analogous reasoning.

I have discussed why we love and why love is important to humans. But why do we love some people and not others? Fromm proposed that anybody can love anybody, as long as a person dedicates sufficient effort to loving. Most of us, however, do not love everybody equally. It is obvious why we love our children: there is a strong biological bond from the day they were born or even before. This love is effortless and powerful, typically lasting as long as we live. Understanding why we can love a stranger, a person we have never met before, is less intuitive. Physical attraction often triggers an initial interest in an individual, but it serves only as an opportunity for developing love.

Love at first sight is a misnomer, because while we may become infatuated with a new acquaintance (I avoid the phrase *falling in love* here to avoid the confusion with love, which is discussed in chapter 1) based on superficial information, such as physical appearance, we really don't know the person. We essentially fall in love with our *perception* of this person (usually based on our own hopes and desires), which may or may not be confirmed by longer acquaintance. To truly love somebody, on the other hand, typically requires us to get to know a person. It is not accidental that many successful romantic relationships arise in situations where individuals spend a lot of time together: at work, in social clubs, and so on. Through knowledge of a person we may identify the true beauty of that person, something valuable that we want to preserve, protect, and nurture.

Many great thinkers have described the recognition of the transcendent nature of love. Plato surmised that loving a person — in the true, ideal sense — connects us with *supreme beauty*. Like many after him (including Fromm), Plato believed that only a few — after realizing the superficial nature of physical attraction and after freeing ourselves from the constraints of self-centered thoughts — are capable of reaching this highest state of love. The ideal lover, according to Plato, has gained deep insights into the human existence through knowledge and contemplation, which enable the lover to perceive an absolute, eternal beauty in the beloved. The nature of this eternal beauty remains open to interpretation.

Going back to biology, love may entail the recognition of *goodness* in a person. This goodness or beauty, which may be demonstrated by habits such as kindness, thoughtfulness, and compassion toward others, is a reflection of the goodness in humanity. As these characteristics are favorable for maintaining the species, this makes perfect sense from an evolutionary point of view. Unconscious or conscious recognition of these characteristics in a person may trigger the genetically determined response of what we perceive as love: a strong feeling of affection and the desire to care for this person. Neuroscientists believe the perception of beauty stems from the physical proximity of the brain areas responsible for processing concepts of love and beauty.[20] The recognition of this goodness also affects how the unique characteristics of a person, such as personality and appearance, are viewed. We love the individual person with his or her idiosyncrasies, even though true love itself may be universal.

A broader interpretation of the ideal lover's recognition of beauty in the beloved — and likely closer to Plato's idea — is that it brings awareness of the wonder of life itself and, with that, awe for its creator. In loving, the lover perceives the uniqueness of the beloved and, by extension, the uniqueness of *all* life. We perceive uniqueness as closely related to preciousness and beauty, and, intuitively, we feel the urge to protect what we perceive as treasured. It also becomes intuitive why philosophers and spiritual leaders argue that ideal love extends to *all* life. Fromm believed that a person who does not hold love for all people is not capable of loving any person. The connection between ideal love and spirituality is also easy to understand in this context. If we indeed recognize the beauty in one person as a reflection of the beauty of all life, we are only a short step from applying concepts found in religion, such as the precept to love everybody. Like spiritual and religious practices, the practice of ideal love requires discipline, devotion, and focus, which explains why it is not commonly achieved.

The recognition of beauty is linked to the perception of rarity or uniqueness, but in order to perceive and value someone's distinctive qualities, we generally need to appreciate that person's nature. This explains why we may find it easy to dislike people on the basis of a superficial acquaintance but grow to appreciate them when we spend time together. Fusing our appreciation for somebody's goodness and uniqueness likely increases our perception of beauty in that person.

Ideal love depends on the ability of the lover to perceive the beauty in another person. One person may recognize beauty and uniqueness in somebody, while another may not. Again, it is easier to recognize the unique goodness in people when we know them well. This may be one reason why parental love is so strong. As parents, we typically know our children better than anybody else does, and we see goodness in them while others may not. Remarkably, we can focus on this goodness even if our children have obvious character flaws or when they mis-behave. Mothers of murderers may still love their chil-dren, regardless of their crimes.

Conversely, a person ceases to love if he or she be-comes unable to discern any sign of goodness or beauty in somebody. This, too, is a matter of perception — or, rather, of our inability to recognize goodness. Spiritual figures such as the Buddha and Jesus recognized the goodness in *all* people, which, to them, never ceased to exist. To such masters of love, whether they are religious or secular in their views, the very existence of a person is sufficient to warrant love: they see and value the individ-uality, the uniqueness, in each person. Thus, their love is eternal for all individuals, even those with many flaws. Very few of us are capable of this ideal form of love: we are distracted by people's faults and imperfections. As a result, we tend to restrict our love to only a small number of people — which touches the roots of a fundamental human problem.

Since recognizing goodness and unique beauty in a person depends on our perceptive abilities, individuals come to different conclusions as to who is worthy of love. Typically, someone who displays hostility and aggression will not be perceived as lovable unless a person sees be-yond these attributes and recognizes other qualities. Be-cause discerning hostility appeals to the strong impulse of self-preservation, it can be a difficult habit to overcome. To love our enemies, as Jesus taught, may elevate us to a transcendent state entirely free of doubts and struggles, but it is a practice that is difficult to sustain in contemporary society. Ironically, extremely selfless people tend to be marginalized in Western societies because they often resist conforming to society's norms and pressures. Unless we are willing to live a shorter (albeit potentially happier) life or are willing to tolerate marginalization, we will not feel love toward people who seem to be trying to harm us.

The challenge for most of us is finding the balance between extending love to others and identifying individuals who would take advantage of our love. Ideally, we extend our love as far as we can while still being able to successfully navigate our lives. Success, of course, is subject to wide interpretation, and to some it may simply mean not dying prematurely. Limiting our love may help with a career in a power-driven society, but it is also likely to prevent us from experiencing true, lasting contentment. Spending too much time in the pursuit of material wealth is known to be linked to lower levels of happiness.[21]

Although we readily recognize a focus on money or power as selfish, it is possible to see loving as selfish, too. Those who reject the idea of selfless love like to point out that there are obvious rewards for focusing on love. Indeed, the constellation of motives for loving is interesting. Devoting ourselves to the art of loving with the intent of advancing our own happiness is arguably self-serving. However, as soon as we engage in loving — in its true sense, without seeking reciprocity — we are behaving selflessly. If we don't behave selflessly, we are not truly loving. Therefore, while our initial intention to love may be motivated by the pursuit of our own happiness, the act of loving, by definition, has to be a selfless act. It is a (positive) Catch-22. Even if people initially engage in loving for their own benefit, they benefit only if they act in a truly loving manner (and then — ironically — pay no attention to the rewards). Thus the argument of "psychological egoism" is insufficient to explain or describe ideal love.

Despite the prevalence of the idea of mutual romantic love, reciprocity can never be a condition of love itself. The loving person loves the beauty and goodness in people without asking or needing to be loved in return. Reciprocity is important for relationships, but not for the existence of love as an independent phenomenon. Love does, however, benefit both the lover and those who are loved.

In practice, these contemplations are of only semantic relevance. When we love, we don't have the option of being selfish. We don't love in order to attain happiness: instead, we attain happiness as the result of freeing ourselves from jealousy, greed, and selfishness. We love because we recognize goodness and beauty in an individual, and, through that person, the goodness and beauty in all of humanity — and indeed in any life. We also love ourselves, not because we are powerful or smart but because we are part of the same goodness and beauty.

Can we speak of love when referring to our affection

for animals or other living things? In English we use the word *love* liberally to express a range of emotions and attachments — but are these the same as our love for people? Following the definition of love in this book — *the urge and continuous effort for the happiness and well-being of somebody or something* — we can speak of loving our pets and other animals if we experience the desire and determination to see them joyful and healthy. It may be difficult to accept somebody's affection for a dog as love when the human is merely providing food. On the other hand, somebody who spends hours a day with a dog — going beyond regular care to provide the mental and physical nourishment for the optimal development of a pet — shows persuasive signs of love. As in human relationships, we gain delight from experiencing the happiness and well-being of animals. Consistent with the general principle of love, we recognize goodness and uniqueness in them that we seek to nurture and protect. A similar case can be made for strong, dedicated affection for any life.

3. Love as an Art

An art is a skillful human activity undertaken to express a person's perceptions and emotions. Can love be considered an art? To address this question, we first need to explore the mechanism of loving. How do we generate love in ourselves?

Love can be seen simply as a biological impulse that is unique among our drives because of its significance for human survival. Drives like hunger or thirst are activated in response to internal or external triggers: for example, low blood sugar levels elicit the feeling of hunger. A drive that prompts us to eat is obviously vital to sustaining the functioning of the individual.

The effect of all these drives on our state of mind ceases once we have satisfactorily responded to them, for example by eating in response to hunger or engaging in sex when aroused. Thus, their effect is largely transient and beyond our control. Indeed, people generally view the fleeting nature of the pleasure these drives generate as unsatisfactory. Even our greatest highs don't last. The huge success of a challenging project or business deal may make us euphoric for a while, but eventually that feeling fades. For an athlete who breaks a world record in sports, life goes back to normal a few weeks later. We always retain the sense of satisfaction from an accomplishment, but the joy and excitement do not last. When falling in love, we may feel elated for months, but then even these feelings will fade. To revive them, we repeat the actions that bring us pleasure. Many, if not most, of us are dopamine junkies and keep pursuing activities to give us the temporary highs.

Love is different. Love — as the urge and continuous effort for the well-being and happiness of somebody — is a committed state that is maintained until we no longer see beauty, goodness, or uniqueness in the beloved. In contrast to the fleeting nature of other pleasurable drives, the emotions associated with love — including joy, contentment, and affection — have a *sustained* effect on our state of mind. Unfortunately, because we often allow competing drives to dominate, we don't always enjoy the pleasing emotions arising from love. Herein lies our fundamental problem with love: we easily lose our focus on it and let our minds be distracted. When that happens, our loving feelings are repressed until we regain our focus on love.

A few examples may illustrate this concept. A nine-year-old boy has just smashed an expensive vase while chasing after his brother. The boy's father immediately perceives the impulse of severe anger. This anger results from possessive and territorial instincts, and the father feels the urge to furiously reprimand or even slap the child. His love for his son is entirely suppressed at this moment by the force of the anger drive. But if the father takes a deep breath and, instead of acting on his anger, considers the accidental nature of the event and the boisterous nature of children's play, he can recognize the anxiety, remorse, and distress his son is feeling. The father can then wrap his arms around his son and console him. Both feel the soothing, comforting sensation of love.

In this situation, the father must suppress the impulse of anger to allow love to prevail. While the drive for anger comes on instantaneously and subconsciously, almost as a reflex, the drive for love surfaces only after the father recognizes his anger and actively and consciously rejects it. This concept is critical for understanding the dynamics of loving.

Another example further illustrates the underlying forces of love. A married woman receives sexual advances from a colleague. The woman feels aroused by the advances and perceives the desire to follow her impulse. At that moment, her mind is preoccupied with sexual arousal. When consciously recognizing her excitement, however, she realizes that giving in to her impulse would hurt her partner, whom she loves. Indeed, she would be betraying her effort for her spouse's happiness and well-being. The woman rejects her impulse for sexual activity and refuses the colleague's advances. Once she has done so, she feels love for her spouse. Again, she must actively reject a competing impulse in order to allow love to have its effect.

Another very common scenario is finding it difficult to act in a loving way when we are hungry. Here again, the influences of different essential drives collide. Many people are irritable and may even lash out at others when hungry but return to their regular, caring selves once they have eaten.

Recognizing the mechanisms of loving, it becomes clear why our actions are often *not* motivated by love. At any given moment, self-serving motivations may conflict with and dominate the urge to love: the drives to eat, drink, or have sex; the drive to secure our material well-being by going to work or grocery shopping; the urge to maintain our status as a potential mating partner by grooming, dressing up, or working out; the quest to attain higher social status by pursuing power, wealth, and fame; or the urge to amuse and entertain ourselves. Some of these activities are functional: that is, we perform them out of necessity, without gaining much enjoyment from them. Others are immediately rewarded with some level of pleasure or satisfaction.

Because yielding to many self-serving impulses brings instant gratification, they have a strong effect on human behavior. Like all mammals (and probably most other living beings), we are attracted to activities that give us positive reinforcement. In other words, we are pleasure driven. We enjoy eating because it produces a pleasant sensation. We crave sex because it gives us satisfaction. We use intoxicants to give us a pleasant buzz.

Even small rises of dopamine are very alluring. Researchers have found that interacting with others on social media shares similarities with chemical addictions because we crave the little jolts of excitement that come from receiving new messages and "likes."[1] Conversely, not receiving such feedback from our social-media platforms may reinforce the urge to seek it. Research also shows that revealing information about ourselves, as we often do on social media, triggers reward centers in the brain, reinforcing the behavior.[2] No wonder many of us spend hours each day hunched over our electronic devices.

Our strong drive for pleasure often overrides any conscious reflections. We know that it is harmful to eat or drink too much, yet many people do. We know that unprotected sex may put us at risk of infections, yet many people ignore those concerns. On the other hand, we are hesitant about engaging in activities that require effort, even if they are associated with rewards. We know that regular exercise is good for us and that it can produce some level of euphoria, yet many people struggle with getting enough exercise, as the ratio of effort to reward seems unfavorable. In general, we seek maximum pleasure from minimal effort.

Given the many and conflicting motivations flooding our minds and the strong allure of activities yielding short-term pleasure, a sustained focus on loving thoughts and deeds is difficult to maintain. Adding to the challenge, concentrating on long-term love — in contrast to the excitement of early infatuation — is rewarded with sensations of contentment but typically not with the elation associated with spikes of high dopamine or corticoid steroid release.

Thus, in rejecting the impulse for short-term gratification, we have to weigh the loss of short-term highs against the serenity, purpose, and fulfillment that result from loving. We need to consciously or subconsciously prioritize love over competing impulses. Doing so does not mean we can't do anything else. Many functions of daily life still need to be performed. But we perform them without losing our focus on love.

Essentially everything we think and do can be done with love in mind. However, to be aware of this every minute of every day is enormously hard. Unless we were raised to focus on love, it requires extensive training of our brain. That is why Erich Fromm considered love an art — and I agree.

To master the art of love, we must remain focused on love and reject competing impulses. Like any demanding skill, it takes considerable time, practice, and focus. Many struggle to learn it well, and only a few become expert.

For most of us, it's easy to stay focused on love when our minds are not challenged by other strong drives. Everybody knows the feeling of wanting to kiss the entire world when something exciting happens, like completing a marathon or having a baby. We typically feel empathetic and generous in these moments because our egotistic drives are satisfied and not competing with the drive to love.

By the same token, it is easier to be loving when our minds are not preoccupied with work problems, how to pay the rent, or other survival challenges, because such worries trigger potentially hostile survival instincts.

Even under the best of circumstances, it requires an enormously disciplined mind and typically years of training to focus on love all the time. As with all brain processes, the practice of loving may be conscious or unconscious. In the learning phase, our active involvement in loving may require conscious effort. Eventually, however, it becomes second nature. We don't have to identify and reject our egotistic impulses anymore: they lose their power over us, and we are naturally guided by our concern for others.

To some people, being consistently loving comes effortlessly. It is conceivable that such people have inherently less pronounced egotistic and competitive drives that allow their compassionate impulses to prevail. Others may have had parents who taught them in childhood to suppress egotistic thoughts and actions. As a result, these individuals may have learned to prioritize loving without being aware of it.

The challenge of maintaining a focus on love helps explain our fascination with *falling* in love. Not only is this state of mind associated with unparalleled elation, but it is entirely effortless! We don't have to do anything to fall in love. It just happens, often unexpectedly. No wonder we perceive falling in love as magical: we feel totally changed from one moment to another without doing a thing.

Falling in love results from a combination of factors, some inherent and some cultural, triggered by physical and emotional attraction to somebody. Like most human drives, the effects of falling in love come about without our active involvement. And as with most of those other human drives, the sensations associated with falling in love eventually cease: they last only until they have fulfilled their (evolutionary) purpose.

In contrast, actual love does not cease unless we let it. While falling in love is a *passive* phenomenon, actual love generally requires our *active* focus on love and our active rejection of competing impulses. This explains why we resist discounting falling in love as mere infatuation and are tempted to equate it with true love. Wouldn't it be nice if true love were the powerful force seen in the movies, which simply comes over us and lasts forever?

Love is indeed an amazing and powerful force, but we don't get it for free. Like most great things in life, we have to earn it, by training our minds to reject competing impulses. Our drive to love seems to be the default setting of our mind. If we remove egotistic impulses, love will take their place. The cliché of loving from the bottom of your heart holds true in the sense that you find love if you remove all the other stuff.

If art is considered a uniquely human activity, is love uniquely human, too? There is evidence of loving behaviors among animals, particularly primates. These behaviors, however, appear to be passive and instinct driven. Certain situations and activities may activate the love impulse in animals to foster mating and socialization. While there are numerous examples of animals exhibiting apparently altruistic behavior, it is doubtful whether animals have the awareness to actively focus on love and reject competing drives after rational contemplation. Likely, this ability is uniquely human, a result of our highly evolved cortical brain function.

It is conceivable that the ability to control egotistical impulses, as happens with love, substantially contributed to the reproductive success of the human species. Despite wars and cultural conflicts, more than seven billion humans cohabit largely peacefully on this planet. In times of crisis or natural disaster, such as an earthquake, a wave of solidarity sweeps around the world and elicits help and support from many sources. Daily news accounts of atrocities committed by a few people obscure the fact that the vast majority of humans are compassionate. We do not sufficiently acknowledge the effect of human love on our history.

4. Self-Love

I n the definition of love as the *urge and continuous effort for the well-being and happiness of somebody,* the somebody is usually assumed to be another person — but what about us? Self-love is the recognition that we are loving, respectful, and considerate individuals. Yet self-love sounds like an oxymoron because we typically associate love with selflessness.

Saint Thomas Aquinas identified self-love as the root of sin.[1] We have to distinguish, however, between selfishness and self-love. Selfishness involves serving our own desires and interests without regard to anybody else's needs. Self-serving thoughts and actions may indeed hinder our ability to love. They are often detrimental to relationships, to society, and ultimately to our own well-being. Resisting self-serving impulses may lead us to a state of inner contentment and happiness. Self-love, by contrast, does not serve selfish impulses: it implies self-acceptance. Love for ourselves is not fundamentally different from love for others. At its core is the recognition of goodness and beauty in us that needs to be nurtured and preserved. Self-love, therefore, is directed at supporting our own happiness and well-being and recognizing our own uniqueness and value.

Recognizing our own uniqueness and loving ourselves is critically important for our ability to love others and to maintain stable relationships. If we don't love ourselves, we have difficulty accepting others' love for us as sincere. To allow others to love us, we must consider ourselves worthy of receiving love. Acceptance of and contentment with who we are is essential to our ability to mature, and Fromm asserts that only a mature person — one who has overcome the early developmental stage of narcissism — is able to truly love.

A person who struggles with self-acceptance is susceptible to stress. Subconsciously considering ourselves as not deserving of love causes us to incessantly seek affirmation and reassurance of our value. This causes the mind to release stress hormones, which may be associated with conscious anxiety. In addition, this search for affirmation, which is critical to our well-being, is an impulse that competes with love. As a result, people with poor self-esteem may have difficulties focusing on love and maintaining relationships. Their need for affirmation often dominates their thoughts and actions, making them less attentive to the needs of their partners.

Conversely, in the desire to elicit affirmation from a

partner, some people may overcompensate and smother the partner with affection. Furthermore, poor self-esteem may provoke jealousy. If we believe others are more lovable than we are, we may constantly fear that a partner will leave us for somebody else, and jealousy (most likely unjustified) may have a devastating effect on a relationship.

Self-love requires a mature perception of ourselves and freedom from anxiety to meet parental or societal expectations. Unfortunately, our self-image may be substantially influenced by such expectations, with detrimental consequences for self-acceptance. Every person acquires beauty by being unique, an individual. Every person holds goodness in the form of an ability to love. Realizing these facts allows us to accept and love ourselves. If, on the other hand, we are convinced that our value as a person derives from becoming successful by external standards, we set ourselves up for conflicts.

My personal experience may illustrate this point. My father — a physician and academician — had very high expectations for my academic performance for as long as I can remember. He repeatedly made it clear that he valued people by their academic achievements. I recall regular knowledge quizzes at the dinner table and my father's dismissive attitude if I failed to give the correct answers. My report cards were met with similar disapproval if they did not show the highest grades and accolades. Since they often did not, my father grew increasingly skeptical of my academic potential. He did not act this way with malicious intent — he probably set the bar high to motivate me — but it had a negative effect on my self-image.

Subconsciously, I became very insecure about my academic ability. Driven by the desire to prove my intellectual worth — and thus demonstrate to my father my value as a person — I pursued an academic career. Often, though, I found myself ridden with doubt as to whether I truly belonged in academia. Any test or performance evaluation was highly stressful for me because academic approval was critical to my sense of self-worth. It took me many years to understand that my value as a person was dependent not on my academic performance but on my uniqueness and my ability to love.

The pivotal moment for me was when I was considering proposing to Denise, who is now my wife. My optimal career path would have required me to move across the country: I had to decide whether to follow that path or to compromise for personal reasons. After some soul-searching about my life's purpose, I realized that I wanted my identity to be defined not by my career but by family — by love. More than anything else, I wanted the family that I never had. Understanding my value as a person independent of my work not only reduced my job-related stress but also led me to embrace my profession without the burden of my father's or my own expectations. Although I might have entered this career for the wrong reason, I discovered, luckily, that academia was a very good choice for me after all.

Feeling pressure to fulfill parental expectations is common. Parents' ambitions for a child's future may heavily influence the child's sense of self-worth. Seeing ourselves as deserving of love is a belief that is typically instilled in early childhood and one that largely depends on our parents' efforts. Lack of attention or denial of approval during childhood often has devastating consequences for a person's self-esteem.[2] A mother who unthinkingly disparages her daughter's physical appearance may plant a seed of self-doubt that takes years to eradicate. Many girls grow up feeling physically unattractive and therefore unworthy of love because of misperceptions instilled by an environment that heavily emphasizes superficial perfection. When parents fail to assure their children of their love and approval, they make their children vulnerable to seeking affirmation elsewhere.

Peers and society may also exert enormous pressure on individuals to meet certain criteria for success and thus may influence their perception of self-worth. The importance attached to power, professional advancement, and material gain in our society may be at least partly grounded in the subconscious desire to feel good about ourselves. Power and wealth signal that we deserve to be respected and valued.

That is not to say that everybody striving for material gain is driven by unresolved self-esteem issues. Ambition and desire for power are also intrinsic impulses with evolutionary benefits. Competitiveness has resulted in many socially beneficial achievements, such as progress in science and technology, and it may appear intuitive to foster an environment that stimulates and supports individual achievement. Ultimately, however, it depends on what values a society prioritizes. Some may favor a society that focuses on developing harmonious relationships between people rather than on progress in science and technology. Such a society may offer less comfort and convenience but may be more closely aligned with humans' intrinsic nature and thus offer greater contentment. Most modern Western societies, however, place the highest value on material gains and social status.

Children who suffer a lack of attention and approval may develop into adults driven to prove to others — particularly to parents — that they are winners. While directing our energy toward professional success may be beneficial for our society, it detracts from our ability to recognize and correct a potential inner imbalance. Highly influential and powerful people in our society often exhibit unfavorable personality traits that may impair their personal relationships and happiness. In a study of 147 U.S. college graduates, the pursuit of extrinsic values, such as income and status, was associated with lower personal satisfaction than was a focus on inner growth and relationships.[3]

Love requires effort and dedication. A person who spends sixteen hours a day promoting a business will have little time left to devote to a spouse, children, or friends. Conversely, a person who realizes that love and attention are not dependent on wealth or status will be more inclined to dedicate time and effort to loving others than to personal achievement.

Accepting ourselves as lovable because of our individuality and capacity to love reduces our need to seek affirmation and frees up energy to devote to love. A mind that is not controlled by self-serving impulses is a peaceful, contented mind. This is the state of happiness sought by philosophers and spiritual practitioners.

This is not to say that attending to our own needs is frivolous: it is important for our well-being. If we neglect the needs of our bodies and minds, we will be unable to give love to others. The body enables us to be who we are, and we need to appreciate the wonderful functions it performs for us. In return, it is our responsibility to care for our body as best we can by being attentive to our diet and our need for exercise, as well as by protecting it from environmental harm. If we do not love our body, we will not care for it adequately.

The key to a balanced personality is...balance. Too little attention to ourselves makes it difficult for us to function in society and in life. Too much attention to ourselves has a similarly detrimental effect.

How do we strike this balance? The answer is different for each person. Some are content with giving much and taking little, and for others the opposite is true. One key to happiness is to balance activities that offer instant gratification with the constant, active pursuit of love. Focusing on short-term satisfaction leaves us feeling hollow once the excitement has passed. By cultivating a loving mind, however, we can relish amusements while never falling into that hole of anticlimax. Knowing ourselves and where we strike that balance helps us convey realistic expectations to our partners. Realizing our strengths and limitations allows appropriate judgment of our abilities and actions.

Unfortunately, it can be very difficult for people to recognize their own lack of self-esteem and even harder to correct it, because it may be subconscious and not immediately accessible through reflection. Correcting negative perceptions of ourselves developed in childhood may require many years of effort, yet most of us live hectic lives that allow little time for such introspection. Curiously, we hardly know ourselves.

Introspection and reflection, possibly directed by a psychologist or other trained mental health practitioner, are valuable tools for finding inner balance. The longer we ignore or are oblivious to our poor self-esteem, the harder it is to correct it. Like loving others, learning to love ourselves requires work and dedication; but it ranks among the most important endeavors in life. There is plenty of excellent material available on this topic.[4]

The most important step is becoming aware of our state of mind. Honest, self-critical introspection may help us assess how our self-esteem affects our relationships. The perspective of a close friend or family member can be of great help. But before embarking on love for others, we must recognize the importance of developing a mature mind. Ultimately, it comes down to how we want to define ourselves. People often speak of the legacy they will leave in this world. If we want to be defined by our careers, we may have trouble finding lasting happiness in relationships. If we want our lives to be defined by love, we are already on the road to happiness.

5. Love and Romantic Relationships

Until now, I have focused on the phenomenon of love as the urge and continued effort for the happiness and well-being of somebody — but not a specific person. In its ideal form, love is directed at *all* people, recognizing the goodness and beauty in everyone. In real life, however, we often fail to recognize these attributes in people. Instincts aimed at self-preservation prompt us to apply our love selectively, typically to a limited circle of family and friends. Furthermore, we commonly restrict romantic love to even fewer people. We may love our friends and family members, but we typically consider these forms of love different from the love we have for our partner. Is romantic love indeed different from any other love?

The term *love* is frequently used as a synonym for romantic relationships, but love and relationship are not the same: indeed, distinguishing between them is critical. Individuals sometimes continue to feel love for partners even after separation or divorce. If two people realize that their differences are too substantial to allow adequate growth in a relationship, they may agree to go different ways but still feel love for each other. On the other hand, there are couples who don't love each other but maintain a marriage or similar relationship for economic, social, or religious reasons. Though married and living under one roof, they may live quite separate lives without even feeling much regard for one another. Other people may feel love for one another without ever entering a romantic relationship. A relationship between two (or more) individuals has its own complexity and dynamics, which are important to recognize. Love in romantic relationships is not fundamentally different from love in other contexts, but romantic love is paired with other aspects of a romantic relationship: passion and sexual attraction.

Most commonly, we assume that romantic relationships involve two partners. However, high rates of infidelity and divorce in Western countries may raise the question of whether romantic love has to be monogamous and whether monogamy is our natural form of partnership. The origin of monogamy is intensely debated, but at least in Western societies, its prevalence has been strongly influenced by Judeo-Christian religious traditions. There is evidence that monogamy was a common mode of human family organization as long as twenty thousand years ago.[1] However, several sociological and evolutionary theorists have argued that it has never been the predominant form of partnerships in human history. Today, polygamy is practiced particularly in Africa and parts of Asia.[2] In monogamous societies, many practice serial monogamy — that is, sequential relationships with different partners. As long as those involved are indeed devoted to the happiness and well-being of all partners, both monogamy and polygamy can be loving relationships.

A nonromantic relationship is mainly supported by love and attachment. A romantic relationship also involves love and attachment (and often a stronger commitment than a nonromantic relationship), but, in addition, it commonly includes passion and sexual attraction. These components represent distinct human drives that may be active to very different degrees at different times during a relationship.

Passion, in this context, refers to the intense emotions of the falling-in-love phase, which typically is confined to the first months or years of a romantic relationship. This phase is characterized by high levels of excitement and infatuation triggered by surging levels of certain blood hormones. Sexual attraction also typically manifests itself early in a romantic relationship. Although it may build somewhat over time, it tends to decline eventually. The waning of either passion or sexual attraction may cause conflicts between partners, particularly if they don't anticipate these changes.

Love and attachment, on the other hand, commonly develop somewhat later in the relationship and may increase over time. Attachment is an impulse, along with love, sexual attraction, or aggression. The drive for attachment — like that for love — functions to build bonds between individuals, which support both the individuals' and the species' survival. Attachment does not require conscious involvement: it is a passive feeling triggered by the comfort derived from common experiences and routines with a person or group. Attachment may foster a strong tie between people, including the desire for regular contact.

We have all experienced the phenomenon of missing familiar people, pets, and objects when we are separated from them. The longer the time spent together and the more intense the positive memories, the stronger the feelings of attachment. An important difference between attachment and love is that we may develop attachments even to persons or situations that we don't particularly like. There may be a grouchy, long-serving colleague at work who is kind of a loner, does not participate in social activities after work, and is not very popular. Yet after he retires, many coworkers might say that they miss his grumpy presence. Familiarity is comforting to us, and conversely, the removal of some familiar element in our lives is unsettling.

Attachment is frequently the reason partners maintain a relationship despite not loving each other anymore. They still share the comfort of familiarity, which may be quite strong after many years spent together and fond memories. Couples often find it hard to give up this comfort and may even mistake their feelings of attachment for love, which in turn may lead to continuing a relationship without the presence of actual love.

A romantic relationship involves several human drives, typically including passion, sexual attraction, love, and attachment. In general, the intensity of these feelings shifts over time. Passion and sexual attraction often run high in the early years of a romantic relationship and then decline. Love and attachment, on the other hand, develop over time and help sustain a relationship in the long run. Figure 1 depicts the shift of the major drives in relationships over time based on trends in longitudinal studies.[3] (The scale and magnitude of changes are provided solely for illustrating the concept and are not based on specific data.)

Figure 1: Intensity of Romantic Relationship Factors over Time

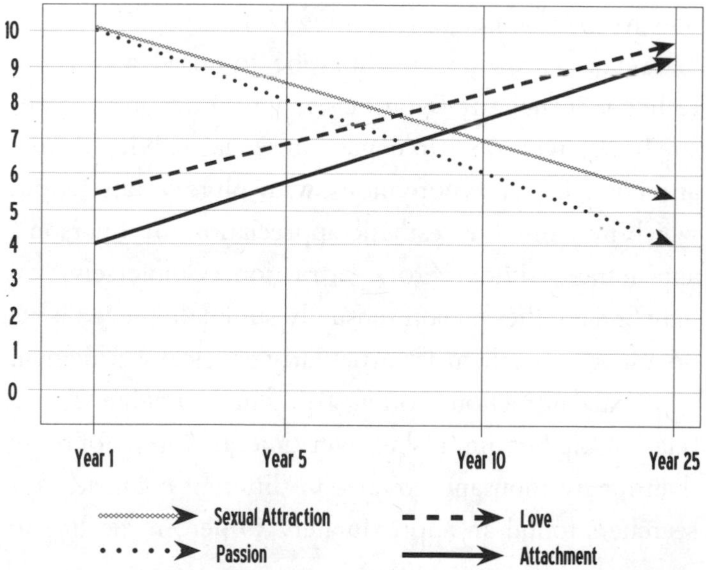

The dynamics of these drives may vary greatly from relationship to relationship and from person to person. Some romantic relationships may initially be based on friendship and then develop into passion and sexual attraction. Other relationships may involve little passion but develop into strong love and attachment. Still others may be based on sexual attraction before love and attachment develop.

The meaning of emotions in a romantic relationship may be tremendously confusing. The mistaking of passion for actual love is one of the most common misperceptions in romantic relationships. Couples are often disappointed when they don't feel intense longing for each other after two or three years of courtship. Indeed, many separate at that time in the belief that their love has ended. They often seek excitement in a new relationship, only to find that this is not lasting either.

Sexual attraction, too, may be confused with other feelings. Sexual attraction or sex appeal denotes the desire between partners to engage in sexual activity. Sexual attraction is not synonymous with physical attraction, which may involve aesthetic appreciation for a person's appearance without erotic attraction. Conversely, we may find another person sensually stimulating even if we do not perceive them as particularly physically attractive.

Sexual attraction is often strong in the beginning of a relationship but diminishes over time. In a study of more than ninety thousand couples in different countries, researchers found an approximately 50 percent decline in the rate of sexual intercourse among long-term married couples (married thirty years or more), compared to that of newly wedded partners.[4] In research on more than three thousand U.S. adults, the partners' level of satisfaction with marital sex was inversely related to the duration of marriage.[5] Again, experience varies widely: some couples enjoy high-quality sex even after decades of marriage. But waning sexual attraction between couples is a major reason for discontent in a relationship, which may trigger infidelity and a breakup.

Another complication is that partners may experience different degrees of shifts in their feelings. For example, one partner may still be highly sexually attracted to the other, while the second partner no longer feels attracted. Maintaining a happy romantic relationship over many years is challenging because of these potential conflicts and evolving dynamics.

The critical component — the glue — of the relationship is love. While passion, sexual attraction, and attachment are largely passive drives that occur without much active involvement on our part, love requires our active participation. In an ideal relationship, each partner provides a continuous, committed effort for the well-being and happiness of the other. Love itself is selfless, and if both partners have mastered the art of loving, the ebbing of passion and sexual attraction will not weaken their relationship. In fact, love may positively influence the effect of these drives.

Unfortunately, few people master the art of loving,

and many of us are strongly influenced by the force of competing, mostly self-serving, drives. It is common for people to see relationships as an exchange market, expecting parity and a specific return on investment: "If I do this and that for you, I should get this and that back." Another common basis of disagreement is different expectations of what partners will receive in return for their contribution to a relationship.

Love does not ask for love in return. Relationships, in general, do. If we keep giving love and don't receive any in return, the relationship will suffer. If we feel unloved by our partner, our desire and ability to maintain the partnership may conflict with our natural desire for our own happiness.

In an ideal world, we would be able to focus solely on our love for others. But human beings have requirements that are essential for our physical and emotional health. If we were entirely selfless, we would die of dehydration within a few days, because we wouldn't follow our drive to drink water. Love for others has to be balanced against requirements for our own well-being and happiness.

The key word here is *balance*. Individuals have different views of how much attention they should devote to self versus others. In relationships, these views may clash. For example, a spouse may consider it essential to her or his happiness to watch TV all evening after work, but this places a burden on a partner who takes care of the children at the same time. True love for a partner should require the spouse to critically reflect on this "need."

Doesn't the partner also need a break? A true lover will not only make sure that the beloved gets that break: she or he will do it gladly, as a means of promoting the happiness of the partner. The loving partner, meanwhile, will also make sure the spouse gets to watch some TV. Between two truly loving partners, there will be no conflict, as each strives to promote the other's happiness simultaneously and continuously.

More commonly, the partners' attention to each other's happiness is subordinated to satisfying their own needs and desires. This is often because partners are simply unaware of or complacent about how to maintain a happy partnership. We learn how to build and maintain relationships all our lives. Growing up, we observe the partnership between our parents (or the lack of it), make friends in and outside school, and begin dating. From these interactions, some of us learn (and some don't) that happy partnerships require a balance between give and take. If one partner only takes and the other one only gives, the partnership is likely to fail or turn into an unhealthy, possibly abusive situation.

A romantic relationship is a partnership that is more intense than other relationships, loaded with expectations and additional dynamics (such as passion and sex). However, the key principles of relationships apply — and matter even more.

Some believe everything in a relationship will be different and easier when people are in love. This is typically true in the beginning of a relationship, when we are under the influence of euphoria-producing hormones. It still can be true later on, if we maintain our focus on love. The problem is that we often let our focus slip and allow other things, as trivial as watching TV, to become more important.

Happy partners keep a close eye on each other's contentment all the time. That does not mean we cannot pursue enjoyable activities without our partner. A loving partner will encourage us to pursue our own activities and interests. Again, the key is balance. The balance point is not the same for all couples, and it is not always obvious. While loving partners don't keep track of how much they do for one another, a relationship in which one partner consistently compromises more than the other is not balanced.

The loving person minimizes his or her own needs and gladly devotes effort toward the well-being and happiness of the beloved. However, receiving love is also essential for our emotional well-being. We typically enter a relationship with the expectation of gaining affection, comfort, support, and more. Knowing that another person recognizes our individuality and goodness affirms our sense of self-worth. Love is a source of strength, trust, and peacefulness. When we feel loved, we feel free and secure. We enjoy the sense of union. We know there is somebody looking out for us. We can drop our guard and be ourselves without fear of getting hurt. We don't have to prove anything: somebody who loves us has already recognized the *goodness* in us.

Maintaining a romantic relationship over many years requires managing competing interests and potential differences in personalities, expectations, and levels of commitment. In romantic relationships, we constantly experience impulses opposing or at least competing with our intention to love. Every day we face pressures from work, economic worries, health concerns, personal ambitions, family issues, and other social contacts and obligations. We may sometimes perceive these matters as more important than our goal of loving.

Most of us have to work hard to make a living and run a household. We often spend our leisure time watching television, reading, playing video games, or engaging with social media — activities that are not necessarily conducive to our personal growth or to nurturing what should matter most: our relationship with our partner. Maintaining a strong love for a partner requires an active effort to prioritize love over competing matters.

The choice, which we face many times each day, is to identify what matters to us most. A focus on the relationship leaves room for many loving gestures and activities even in the busiest schedule. Maintaining this focus on love becomes more challenging with the number and gravity of competing interests. In the extreme case, illness and pain may diminish a person's ability to focus on love and other matters, as self-preserving impulses may dominate. Yet these situations often present an opportunity to refocus on the most important things in life, and people find themselves once again prioritizing love over other matters. Economic hardship, like illness, may compel us to focus on self-preservation. It is therefore not surprising that failure of romantic relationships tends to be more common among couples of lower socioeconomic status.[6]

When couples in successful long-term relationships are asked about their secrets, they typically give answers like "Respect one another," "Be attentive to your partner," and "Work as a team." All these phrases are expressions of love, the urge and continuous effort for the happiness and well-being of somebody.

Knowingly or unknowingly, partners in successful long-term relationships find ways to continuously support each other's joy in life. My parents-in-law had been married for fifty-two years when my father-in-law died. My wife, Denise, once asked her dad about the secret of her parents' happy marriage. My father-in-law said: "It's really simple. There is nothing in the world important enough to me to be worth upsetting your mother. If you find somebody who shares this attitude, you won't have any trouble with your marriage."

This simple but immensely profound statement expresses the key element of the art of loving: prioritizing the happiness of somebody over other impulses you may have. It acknowledges that there are other things in life that are of interest and importance to us but declares that love must take priority over these things.

The other critical aspect of this statement is its unconditional nature: it applies to *all* circumstances, and *nothing* ever justifies upsetting our partner. It is easy to be considerate when we feel amiable, but it may be hard when we are irritated or stressed. Coming home after a rough day at work and noticing that the kids have made a big mess in the living room may cause some people to take their anger out on the family. Our partner may do something that irritates us. Whatever the challenge may be, we have the power to reject the negative impulse. It is our choice. If the happiness of a partner is a priority, we will reject the impulse of anger because we maintain a focus on love. If two people share this attitude, their relationship will be happy.

Herein lies a big problem with relationships: it takes two! While each of us has power over our actions and our love for others, we cannot control others' love or their actions. We cannot control relationships. Unfortunately, we may be quick to point out our partner's deficiencies but fail to critically inspect our own. When troubles arise, it is always good to start by looking at ourselves. If we are sure we are being as loving as we can be but our partner is not, we need to talk. We may show our love in ways that are intuitive to us but are not understood by our partner, and vice versa. Not only is inquiring about our partner's happiness vital for good communication, but it also directly conveys our love.

There are situations, however, in which a partner is not willing or able to return our love, despite all our efforts and patience. If this is truly the case, we may be better off accepting the situation and moving on. Not all relationships can be salvaged. All our dedication and most serious effort may not be enough if our partner is not genuinely committed to making it work.

Romantic relationships that are destined to last typically require what Fromm referred to as mature personalities, which have passed the developmental stages of narcissism. In general, we are much more influenced by self-serving impulses when we are young, and we develop a more altruistic view with time. It makes evolutionary sense that during their youth, individuals should be primarily concerned with looking out for themselves. Sadly, however, many individuals reach emotional maturity late, or not at all, and this is one reason that romantic relationships frequently fail.

With a mature personality come sensible expectations. It is unrealistic to expect the exhilarating feelings of falling in love to last for more than two to four years. If such expectations nevertheless prevail, the disappointment and misinterpretation when those feelings fade may lead an immature couple to separate. If either partner is primarily self-interested, a partnership cannot work. Each partner must have the best interest of the other in mind and must care for, respect, and nurture the other. Therefore, the most critical question for a new relationship is whether *both* partners have the maturity to understand the dynamics of a partnership — particularly the importance of a continuous effort to promote the happiness of the partner.

Unfortunately, partner selection is often influenced by other criteria, such as appearance and status. Swayed

by these traits, we may overlook obvious red flags or op-
timistically view them as issues from the past. The strong
emotions associated with falling in love are particularly
prone to distort our view of a partner: this sort of "love"
is indeed blind.

Furthermore, some people tend to select partners on
the basis of unresolved psychological issues, such as low
self-esteem or childhood conflicts.[7] Children who experience sexual assault often have trouble with adult relationships, because the mechanisms they develop to deal
with the assaulter, such as submissiveness, may continue
to operate until the issues are addressed. Consequently,
adult survivors of sexual assault in childhood may seek
dominant partners, and this choice brings the risk of recurrent abuse. Less severe trauma in childhood can also
affect our ability to extend trust to others and thus to enter
healthy relationships. A controlling father or mother may
lead a person to select partners likely to perpetuate these
unhealthy relationship patterns. To avoid repeated poor
choices in selecting partners, we must reach a level of
psychological development that allows us to recognize
and address these underlying problems. It is possible to
develop such insight during a partnership if we are open-
minded and motivated to engage in self-improvement.
Unfortunately, this is not always the case.

A common cliché is that opposites attract. Psychol-
ogists have indeed found that we tend to select partners
with character traits complementing our own. Shy, intro-
verted people often pair with partners who are outgoing

and social. Conversely, one study suggests that if partners are too similar, their relationship is less likely to last.[8] Of course, these also are general findings: many couples in happy long-term relationships may see themselves as very much alike.

Most of us don't want to take chances on the success of our partnership and would like to have evidence for strong partnership traits in the other person before marrying or entering into a committed relationship. What should we look for in a partner? Positive signs include a consistent display of consideration for others, knowledge and confidence in a personal vision of life, ability to reflect critically on personal traits, and a record of meaningful romantic and other relationships. In general, people who are genuinely kind and gentle to others, sensitive and considerate, respectful and tolerant, fit the description.

It is also important to know whether these traits will stand up to challenges. We need to know a person for a while to observe their reactions in adverse circumstances as well as happy ones. It has been said that if you want to get to know somebody, you should take a trip together. Spending several days in an unfamiliar environment may reveal a person's true self. There is no substitute for time, however. Rushing into marriage after a few weeks or months of dating typically does not allow us to experience the full spectrum of a person's character and may lead to unpleasant surprises down the road. Solid knowledge of a person is important before making a commitment to a relationship.

Our potential partner may subject us to the same scrutiny. We may increase our chances of finding a compatible mate when we allow our caring, sensitive traits to show. Most people don't like a person who brags about accomplishments, wealth, or status. Conversely, humility and genuine interest in another person are attractive.

Physical appearance is often overemphasized. While physical attraction is typically an important component of romantic relationships, the perception of a person's physical attractiveness is greatly influenced by the recognition of their goodness. A person considered beautiful by conventional standards may be perceived as unattractive if he or she is emotionally cold. Conversely, a kind and warm person is typically perceived as more attractive than when viewed purely by physical characteristics.

An overemphasis on physical attractiveness may be interpreted as representing a lack of maturity and self-confidence. Somebody interested in a committed partnership may be concerned that a person preoccupied with external characteristics may not recognize the importance of inner beauty.

If we have developed a realistic sense of ourselves, we know our strengths and weaknesses. Most important, we have recognized our own uniqueness and that of every other person, and this recognition instills in us respect, humility, and love — for ourselves as well as others. Consequently, we feel confident about who we are and what we want. We don't have to pretend anything to win somebody over. By the same token, this understanding enables us to avoid feeling rejected if somebody chooses another person as partner over us. Self-confidence allows us to accept others' choices without it affecting our perception of our own value.

People have many different ways of communicating and interpreting expressions of love, and understanding these is essential to maintaining a happy relationship. Gary Chapman introduced the concept of the five love languages, categorizing five common ways of conveying love to a partner: words of affirmation, spending quality time together, offering gifts, performing acts of service, and physical touch.[9] He emphasizes that partners may misread one another's actions and intentions because they have different ways of expressing love. The most common example, now almost a cliché, is the case of the husband who works very hard to be able to buy gifts for his wife in the belief that they demonstrate how much she means to him, while she is disappointed because, for her, expressing love means spending time together, which they don't do because he works so much. The main principle behind the idea of the five love languages is to *know* our partners and to exercise the effort and consideration for identifying what makes them happy. Only if we pay close attention to our partner's ways and desires will we be able to understand them and do justice to their individuality.

In some instances, it is difficult or even impossible to know what our partner really wants without clear communication. Focus, attention, effort, and communication are the fundamental principles that allow us to make our partner happy.

Love encourages us to do things we may not want to do but are willing to do for the benefit of the loved one. Hardly anybody really enjoys cleaning up after themselves, running errands, doing the dishes, or taking the trash out, but we can derive satisfaction from these tasks if we think of them as lessening our partner's burden. If going to the opera or a football game is particularly enjoyable for our partner, we will go along even if we really don't like the activity. The other person's happiness is a tremendous reward.

Taking the time to do something special for a partner may mean having less time for work, sports, friends, or leisure. Love supersedes the impulses for self-directed interests. However, sometimes we are so caught up in our work and our routines that we take our partner for granted, including the things he or she does for us. It takes effort to remind ourselves that our partner requires our attention and devotion if our relationship is to be happy.

This discussion of focus, effort, and self-sacrifice may not sound very romantic. How about the miracle of the perfect match? Aren't some people made for each other? Well, there are certainly good matches — even extraordinarily good matches. If two people share similar interests and views, similar or synergistic approaches to life, and compatible ideas about sex, children, finances, and so on, it is much easier for them to maintain enthusiasm for each other.

There are also couples who happen to have a very strong, almost obsessive, reciprocal affection. Most of us know stories of lovers who found each other against all odds, despite difficult circumstances and years or even decades of separation. But is this a sign of particularly strong love, or is it the result of a fantasy that became a fixation? Despite our inclination to believe in matches made in heaven, these cases may reflect an exaggerated form of infatuation, possibly triggered by an unusually good match of physical attraction and compatibility. In any case, the same fundamental principles of focus and effort apply to these relationships as to all other romantic partnerships.

This rather sober analysis of love and relationships does not deny their romantic aspects. Individuals who devote themselves to love will never cease to be amazed by its grace and beauty. To share such love with somebody is the ultimate partnership.

Fairytale love does exist. Many couples not only live together for many decades but also truly share their lives, enjoy each other's company immensely, and celebrate the gift of life together. Their "secret" is simple: continuously valuing love above other matters.

6. Love and Sex

How are love and sex related? Both are common components of romantic relationships, but their dynamics are quite different. From an individual perspective, love and sexual desire may even be competing impulses. Both, however, serve the same evolutionary purpose of passing DNA from one generation to the next. While the function of sexual desire is to facilitate the physical transfer of our genetic information to our offspring, love aims at protecting individuals (and their DNA) to facilitate their own reproduction.

Love and sexual desire may exist independently. Many deeply loving relationships have no sexual component. These bonds, often referred to as platonic, can yet be very powerful. Sexual relationships can also exist independently of love. We all know examples of relationships that are purely physical. In some instances, partners actually dislike each other but still enjoy sex together.

Love occasionally has a negative effect on sexual desire, and vice versa. Freud recognized that sex may trigger the impulse of aggression, which conflicts with loving feelings for a partner.[1] Love demands protection and preservation. Aggression — while not necessarily intentionally hurtful — involves feelings opposed to love, such as power and domination. Some individuals indeed have better sex with partners they don't love because they have fewer inhibitions about hurting their partners' feelings with their words and actions. On the other hand, sex among loving partners may have a much more sensual, rewarding character — as expressed in the phrase *making love*.

Men and women may seek different attributes in partners depending on whether they are looking for love or sex. Attributes such as aggressiveness or promiscuity may be appealing to somebody looking for sexual adventures, but they are often not sought after in long-term partnerships. Nevertheless, a relationship based on sex — without love — may sometimes evolve into a loving relationship. After all, it involves two people spending considerable time together and sharing intimacy. Eventually they may get to know each other and enter a partnership.

Sex and love are, however, distinct impulses that should not be confused. Because sex may lead to ecstatic feelings and short-term satisfaction, an associated relationship may be perceived as meaningful although it often does not develop into mature love. Regardless, many people repeatedly seek the excitement and satisfaction of sexual relationships. Fromm argued that such "orgiastic" bonds, if excessive, may be the result of developmental delays or substitutes for emotional connections.

Even so, recreational sex has become a popular leisure activity, facilitated by online dating sites and smartphone applications. As lust, or the impulse for sex, is a strong human drive, people indulge in sex much as they indulge in other impulses, such as feasting or enjoying stimulants. Common among these impulses is the transient nature of the satisfaction they provide. Some cultures and religions, such as Hinduism, regard the pursuit of instant gratification as a passing developmental phase. Eventually most people recognize the temporary nature of the fulfillment and look for more meaningful, lasting satisfaction.

Provided that there is mutual consent between adult partners, there is no ethical concern with frequent sexual engagements, as long as those involved have no expectations beyond sexual satisfaction. Given the strong drive for sex among humans and the undeniable excitement associated with sexual encounters, humans' responses to lust are an important aspect of life.

Since one function of lust is to promote procreation, and the chances of passing on our DNA are increased if we mate with more than one individual, we typically feel lust not for a single partner but rather for a range of individuals who exhibit certain external characteristics or behavior, such as body shape or inviting posturing. These characteristics are largely genetically determined but may be influenced by social mores and behavior patterns.[2] We may feel a stronger lust toward people we do not know — again an evolutionary advantage, as it promotes fusing our DNA with that of multiple partners to create new life, as opposed to the same partner repeatedly. Similarly, people may feel a stronger attraction toward younger adults, whose fertility is generally greater.

Among primates, humans are unusual in that they copulate more than most other species and copulate throughout the reproductive cycle. Such high sexual drive likely contributed to human reproductive success, but it may be a problem for monogamous relationships. Although many long-term couples enjoy fulfilling sex lives, the drive for engaging in sexual encounters with multiple individuals does not abate when we enter a committed relationship: it may even increase as the novelty and excitement of sex with a partner fade.[3] For some, the lure of novelty may grow over time, creating conflicts with a partner. Similarly, as partners age, younger "competitors" may appear more attractive. It is therefore not surprising that many partners in long-term relationships face fidelity problems.

Reliable information about lifetime infidelity rates among couples is difficult to obtain, given the stigma associated with infidelity in Western societies, but most estimates suggest that it occurs in 10 to 40 percent of relationships.[4] In the beginning of romantic relationships, the excitement and passion make it easy to focus lust on the partner. Over time, the passion may wane: this should not be seen as evidence that love has died but rather as a natural phenomenon. If this occurs, frank communication between partners may open possibilities for the improvement of sex in monogamous relationships.

From an evolutionary standpoint, strict sexual monogamy may not be the optimal way to increase a species. Intuitively, it would be more effective for individuals to have several relationships that allow reproduction. Sexual monogamy is comparatively rare among mammals.[5] By contrast, social monogamy — that is, a couple looking after their offspring together — appears advantageous to the species. Thus, while love and sexual desire may stand in conflict at times, both play a strong role in supporting the species' survival.

Taking an abstract, idealistic view of love, we might permit our partner to engage in sexual activities with other people if this would contribute to the partner's happiness. Social movements based on the idea of "free love" have arisen throughout human history, but they probably became most popular during the sexual revolution in the 1960s. While free love works for some people, many, if not most, have trouble consenting to a partner's mating with others, as it strongly conflicts with our territorial instincts and our sense of self-worth. To resolve this conflict and avoid the associated hurt feelings in typical modern romantic relationships, partners have to prioritize monogamy over sex outside the partnership. Lust for other individuals has to be contained and suppressed for the good of a loving relationship.

From a pragmatic standpoint, giving in to lust for other people is shortsighted and typically endangers the partnership as well as the happiness of all those involved. In other words, the benefit of engaging in sexual activities with other partners is generally small compared to the cost of potentially destroying a good relationship.

The satisfaction derived from sex is typically brief compared to the permanent fulfillment of a loving relationship. Thus, it is important to emphasize that the choice to engage in sex outside a relationship is an active decision. Some may feel that the appeal of sex per se, or sex with different partners, is worth the cost.

Others try to have it both ways. Individuals who cheat on their partners often claim that it happened as a result of a spontaneous impulse, without conscious thought. However, the conscious or subconscious decision to engage in infidelity usually is made *before* the opportunity presents itself. In other cases, infidelity is rationalized by pointing to perceived hostile actions by the partner.

Let's review the example of Andreas and Ruth. Their names and story have been modified to retain anonymity, but they are based on true events. Andreas and Ruth had been married for six years and had two young children. Ruth was often exhausted by the time they went to bed, and she was rarely in the mood for sex. Andreas resented her for their inactive sex life, and in his mind this justified the possibility of cheating. After all, it was Ruth's fault. If she consented to sex more often, he would not have been pushed into this situation.

On a business trip, Andreas went out to a bar with some colleagues. After a number of drinks, he started to flirt with a female colleague and invited her back to his hotel room. The next day, he had a bad conscience but blamed his actions on his wife's attitude and on alcohol.

In truth, however, he had no justification for blaming anybody or anything but himself. He acted without love for Ruth: he acted with disrespect and irresponsibility. Had he committed to being a loving partner, he would have seen that Ruth was exhausted because of her sacrifices for their family. He could have tried to take some of the burden off her shoulders. He could have arranged for a weekend alone for the two of them to rekindle their romance. He also could have understood that parents of young children may have different priorities, at least for a while.

Ironically, Andreas was convinced that he had never loved anybody but Ruth. He did not have any feelings for the colleague he slept with. In his mind, the casual encounter happened in a moment of disinhibition, triggered by physical attraction, alcohol, and lust. His case illustrates that mere affection or concern is not necessarily love. Love — again defined here as the continuous effort for the happiness of another person — demands focus and devotion. Even if Ruth never found out, Andreas did something that he knew would deeply hurt his wife. He acted selfishly, without considering the happiness of his loved one.

Sexual desire may be influenced by love. Surveys among couples reveal that satisfaction with marital sex declines when partners feel less loving toward each other.[6]

Often, dissatisfaction with the relationship results in less sex, which in turn increases the probability of infidelity. Thus, a sudden change in the quality or quantity of sex in a relationship may be a sign of a problem that should be addressed. Conversely, love for a partner — and with it, sexual desire — can be restored by conscious effort. Loving attention to a partner promotes an increase in sexual desire in the partner.

Is it possible that Andreas indeed loves Ruth despite what he did? When impulses such as anger, fatigue, or frustration dominate our minds and actions, we may say or do things that do not convey a lot of love. Such episodes do not necessarily mean we feel *no* love for this person. Similarly, when an impulse of lust is paired with an opportunity of intimacy with somebody else, yielding to that impulse may not conclusively indicate a complete lack of love for a partner. It does mean, however, that the person who cheats has not mastered love.

Andreas's love for Ruth was not important enough to him, not sufficiently strong, to contain his self-serving impulses and prevent his infidelity: he lost his focus on love. A person with a great capacity for love recognizes such impulses and controls them. The weaker the focus on love, the easier it is to be distracted by impulses and give in to them. Many people are like Andreas. They may feel some love for their partner, but not enough to control egocentric impulses and withstand challenges.

In life, we generally cannot have it all, and everything comes at a price. A loving relationship is among the most valuable achievements in life, but it requires sacrifice, including the sacrifice of some individual freedom. The excitement of entering new relationships will cease; raising children requires an equitable shouldering of parenting duties. This seems a small price to pay for a life full of love, care, and respect.

7. Love and Gender

Do men and women love differently? Do relationships between men and women inevitably contain imbalances, incompatibilities, and conflicts?

In most societies, assumptions about gender have particularly strong effects on courtship, relationship, and sexual relations. Until recently, most women depended on their families or husbands for financial support. This dependence not only restricted women's options for partnership but also exerted pressure on women to conform to societal standards for public behavior. Promiscuity, for example, has often been tolerated in men but condemned in women. The stereotype of the assertive male seducer who pursues the reluctant, shy woman caused many to assume these roles when courting. In many societies, even today, married women are expected to be submissive to their husbands.

Because women have long been encouraged to suppress their true thoughts and feelings, it was assumed that women have a lower sexual drive than men. Since the male sex hormone testosterone is a critical factor in determining sex drive, this assumption appeared scientifically sound. We now know, however, that physiological processes are complex and highly variable in both men and women. Sex drive is significantly influenced by other factors, such as levels of other blood hormones and hormone receptor density.

Why are stereotypes so pervasive and hard to dislodge? Pattern recognition is an important mechanism of learning. If we observe repeated occurrences in a similar context, our brain remembers these as associations. Unfortunately, such associations may be unreliable. My mother believed in telepathy because she had the impression that she heard from people soon after she started thinking of them. However, her recollections were selective. She acknowledged that she well remembered the occasions when somebody called after she had thought of them, but she did not remember the occasions when nobody called. When she actually paid attention to whether her thinking about a person was consistently followed by contact from that person, she recognized that most of the time, it was not. When somebody did call, she assumed a connection, possibly because she subconsciously wanted one to exist.

Stereotyping is a troublesome form of building associations: we learn (usually from other people) to associate certain behavior or characteristics with groups of people and then assume that these traits are representative of everyone in the group. Stereotyping can be positive as well as negative: we may assert that "old people are wise," or "Asians are hardworking," but such statements still assign common traits to people without considering their individuality. As such, they may disrespect a person's unique characteristics and undermine our efforts to view people for who they are. Stereotyping is thus contrary to our concept of love.

It is believed that stereotyping is the product of a mind pattern associated with adaptive benefits for the species.[1] It probably was beneficial to our ancestors to extrapolate from a bad experience with one lion to be wary of all lions, and not to give the next lion the benefit of the doubt. An important step in eliminating stereotyping, then, is recognizing it as a primitive and flawed thought pattern. It may help to realize that making a distinction between general and specific attributes requires a higher level of intellectual processing and thus represents a uniquely human advance.

At the same time, resisting the instinct to make flawed associations requires active effort, that is, a conscious rejection of the suggested link. Unfortunately, because our judgments are often subconscious, we may be unaware of our biases and think ourselves unprejudiced. A large German study in 2014 found employers more likely to select applicants with German names than those with foreign names despite the applicants' identical qualifications.[2] When confronted, employers denied any conscious discrimination.

The process of detecting bias is similar to that in scientific observations: that is, it may require testing of a hypothesis. If we want to know if our impression that old people are wise is based on truth, we need first to define wisdom in a testable way, and then compare a sufficient number of old to young persons. If we detect no difference between these groups, we have no proof that our initial impression is correct and thus should reject it. If we do detect a difference, we should pay attention to its magnitude. Let's say we find that forty of one hundred old people are wise, but only twenty of one hundred young individuals. While this finding may suggest that older people are more likely to be wise than younger folks, it still means that most old people are not wise, and to assume that they are would be erroneous.

Assigning attributes to people without knowing them reflects ignorance. While it may be difficult to eliminate subconscious prejudice from our minds entirely, we can and should use mindfulness to actively reject bias. Like the continuous effort involved in love, avoiding prejudice and showing proper respect to all human beings require awareness as well as critical reflection on our thoughts and actions. Such an effort is a fundamental requirement of the art of love.

Gendered stereotypes, such as the view that "men are confident" or "women are organized," are still widely propagated. Indisputably, anatomical and physiological distinctions between women and men go beyond differences in reproductive organs and sexual characteristics:

they affect many organs, including the brain. Research studies show that male and female sex hormones have different effects on organ functions. MRI scanning of women's and men's brains has shown noticeable size differences in certain brain regions as well as the connectivity between regions.[3] Varying blood levels of sex hormones have been shown to affect mood, libido, energy, sleep, and other bodily functions.

Given these physiological differences, it may seem that men and women are in some sense programmed to behave very differently. Behavior, however, is the result of exceedingly complex functions and not easily explained by hormones or minor differences in brain structure.[4] Past experiences, perceived expectations, and genetic makeup allow for tremendous variability in individual conduct. Not surprisingly, many commonly assumed associations between biology and gendered characteristics do not withstand scientific scrutiny.

By contrast, socially prescribed gender roles have a major effect on behavior. Girls and boys typically learn in childhood to accept or reject forms of behavior in accordance with social expectations for their gender. In adulthood, it becomes difficult to distinguish learned from inherent behavior patterns. For example, studies suggest that men — in general — tend to exhibit aggressive behavior more than women do. However, these differences diminish when aggressive behavior in private is examined.[5] Researchers conclude that at least some of the observed effect is due to societal expectations that apply to both women and men.

Support for the notion that many of the observed differences in male and female behavior are due to different social expectations comes from studying cultures around the world where gender roles vary substantially from Western norms. Among a small Central African people called the Aka, men and women are raised with essentially interchangeable gender roles. Both men and women hunt, raise children, cook, and plan the next camps, suggesting that social environment, rather than biology, is the predominant modifier of behavior.

A very popular 1990s book titled *Men Are from Mars, Women Are from Venus* reinforced the myth of a huge gender divide in romantic relationships.[6] The author emphasized the importance of reconciling these differences, but instead of relating them to different personalities, he reinforced the use of stereotypes. Since then, survey after survey has found that both men and women come from planet *Earth* — not anywhere else — with relatively small average differences in attitudes to various aspects of relationships.

Recent research on gender differences paints a much more nuanced picture that reveals general but subtle differences in sex drive in certain phases of life.[7] In other words, a woman may have a greater sexual desire than her partner during certain phases in her life, most of the time, or not at all. Similarly, men and women may have attitudes toward relationships that depart from common clichés. We know that many men, contrary to gender stereotypes, are exceedingly sensitive and emotional, while women may be aloof and pragmatic. Some women may like extended periods of coziness after intimacy, while others may prefer being left alone.

A 2013 report analyzed the evidence from several research studies that together involved more than thirteen thousand participants.[8] The authors included evaluations of sexual attitudes and behaviors, mate selectivity, sociosexual orientation, empathy, gender-related dispositions, and intimacy. While they found differences in the average responses from women and men, the variations did not allow researchers to predict responses on the basis of gender. The report debunked the myth of women and men coming from different planets. Not only are women and men not that different, but the differences observed can largely be explained by societal expectations. Moreover, the survey responses have converged over the past decades.

Ascribing behavior or character traits to gender is not only unsound, it is also disrespectful — just like any other prejudice. A man's failure to listen attentively to his partner reflects the ways of this particular person and not of all men. Just because some women like to shop does not mean most like to. Love requires recognizing the uniqueness of each person.

8. Love for Our Children

Love for our children is special and deserves a separate discussion. It has the tremendously important role of instilling self-acceptance and a concept of love in our children. Loving our children is often the easiest love in life. From the day they are born, and often long before, we feel overwhelming affection for them. To many new parents it is a revelation to discover how much love they are capable of.

After years of largely self-directed living during childhood, adolescence, and early adulthood — possibly involving superficial relationships — the birth of a child typically marks a new phase in life, when parents discover the range and implications of their general capacity to love. The feelings toward a child are not dissimilar to the intense sensations we experience when we fall in love romantically.[1] Indeed, many of the same hormones, such as oxytocin, are being released.

In contrast to the sensations associated with falling in love, however, the love for our children does not diminish or cease. We love our children indefinitely. Unlike our affection for romantic partners, which typically requires some focus to maintain, our love for our children often feels effortless. This effortless love is not to be confused with the *relationship* with our children, which may — at times — be quite difficult and arduous. In contrast to our love, our relationship with our children may require specific dedication to sustain.

The notion that loving our children usually takes less effort than loving other people is consistent with evolutionary theory. Transferring DNA to the next generation through mating requires only short-term affection and attention. Raising offspring, on the other hand, mandates many years of devotion. Nature has made it easier by granting parents the capacity to love their children without much effort.

While it appears intuitive that parental love is embedded in our genes, its underlying psychological mechanisms are less clear. The core principle of love likely applies: our love results from our recognition of goodness and beauty in our children — the wonder and magnificence of life. Young children exemplify innocence and purity, which we feel the urge to nurture and protect. Spending time with our children makes us aware of their uniqueness, which reinforces our love and facilitates strong attachment.

It is also conceivable that parents' love for a child

is further augmented by recognizing themselves in the child, through physical or behavior characteristics. This perception allows parents to see their own goodness and beauty reflected. It also conveys a feeling of continuity and thus, in a sense, immortality. The idea that part of us lives on after we die offers a subconscious boost for parental love. As Plato observed, "Through our children we may partake of the future."[2]

Humans are unique among mammals in their expression of parental love. While other mammals cease caring for their offspring when they reach reproductive age, humans remain closely attached to their children all their lives. Many of the biological mechanisms of love and attachment among parents and children, however, are similar in humans and animals. In both, oxytocin and dopamine have been implicated in mediating reward responses from certain brain regions in parents interacting with offspring.[3]

Parental love is often said to exemplify *unconditional* love. The concept of unconditional love often creates confusion, because love, in the purest sense, is always unconditional. In this view, love arises from the very existence of a person and is not dependent on their actions or behavior. For most people, however, the ability to love requires a recognition of goodness and beauty in the other person, and if this perception of goodness is betrayed, love may not last. For parents, the perception of goodness and beauty in our children is firmly anchored in us. A child could do the most horrendous things and still be loved by the parents.

In contrast to love itself, relationships, particularly romantic ones, assume reciprocity of affection. Not receiving love in a romantic partnership may be a valid reason to end the relationship. By contrast, while we might wish that our children love us back, we would not make our love for them conditional on reciprocity; nor would we terminate our relationship with our children if they did not return our love. Thus our bond with our children is an example of an unconditional, loving relationship.

This is not to say that parents may not perceive varying levels of affection for their children, without wavering in their love. Whether we are reprimanding our children for misbehaving or rewarding them with a kiss for fulfilling our expectations, we really don't love them more or less at that moment, but we may express different emotions.

Children often realize much later that parental actions and rules that they originally perceived as hostile, such as curfews, were in fact signs of their parents' love and concern for their safety. It is critical, however, for us to convey to our children that our love and support for them are indeed unconditional, even if we don't always express loving affection.

This point illustrates an important difference between the expression of affection and the phenomenon of love. Expressing affection may reflect our current state of mind or be directed at achieving a purpose: it is a transient condition. Love, by contrast, is an enduring state that may manifest itself in a variety of ways, though always with the goal of the beloved's happiness and well-being. Although children are perceptive, we should seek to ensure they know that our love for them is truly unconditional and not dependent on their actions.

Despite our instinct to love our children, it can be difficult for parents to fully devote themselves to a joyful relationship with their children. The British philosopher Bertrand Russell famously wrote in 1930: "Affection of parents for children and of children for parents is capable of being one of the greatest sources of happiness, but in fact at the present day the relations of parents and children are, in nine cases out of ten, a source of unhappiness to both parties, and in ninety-nine cases out of a hundred a source of unhappiness to at least one of the two parties."[4] Several decades later, our outlook on the relationship between parents and children may be less pessimistic, but problems are still not infrequent.

Many of the reasons for tension between parents and children are the same today as in 1930: parents themselves may have undeveloped personalities with poor self-image, unresolved trauma or conflicts, needy and suffocating characters, controlling dispositions, an unconscious desire to hold power, or an inability to accept love for themselves. These traits prevent them from recognizing and fulfilling their children's need to be loved, despite their best intentions.

If we have not developed self-respect and self-confidence as adults and have not reached a mature understanding of love, we are not fully prepared for parenting. Because children are well aware of our state of mind, our struggles and unhappiness will affect them. Even if we do not feel motivated to resolve these personal difficulties for our own sake, we must strive to do so out of love for our children.

Ideally, before considering having children, we should ask ourselves if we are sufficiently mature and can provide a loving environment. A strong sense of respect and confidence in ourselves as well as our partners will help create a robust foundation for a child's development. Establishing a stable, happy relationship with our partner for several years is also a wise beginning. In an ideal world, we should be confident that our partnership will last at least until the children are grown. We know that children are resilient, and those who grow up in difficult family circumstances may still achieve happiness in later life. However, children may find it much harder to learn how to love if they do not experience love while growing up.

Parents' actions and behavior have a tremendous influence on children's ability to find happiness and love. Their worldview is shaped by ours. The way in which we approach and treat others, and the way we deal with frustration and adversity, will have an enormous impact on how our children experience life. The example we set within the family will form their idea of relationships.[5] If love is an integral part of every family dynamic, children will find it easy and natural to be loving, while those who grow up without love will struggle to come to the same point. Our focus and attention to love are doubly important, as they not only serve our own enlightenment but also affect our children for the rest of their lives.

Growing up with unconditional love enables children to develop confidence that will help them build lives of their own. Lack of loving support, on the other hand, may lead to self-doubt and insecurities. The case of the Moceanu sisters illustrates the effect of parental attitude on children's outlook on life.[6] Dominique Moceanu is a Romanian-born Olympic gold medal–winning gymnast who found out at age twenty-six that she has a younger sister, Jennifer Bricker, who was given away for adoption after being born without legs. Jennifer grew up with foster parents and also excelled in gymnastics, despite her disability. Although the sisters shared success as athletes along with many character traits, Dominique noted a distinct difference: Jennifer brims with confidence in everything she does, while she — like her other sister, Christina — has struggled in this regard. Jennifer was raised with lots of encouragement and support, whereas Dominique and Christina felt "they were beaten down by their father." While they were all extremely successful, Jennifer felt much better about herself — despite her disability — than her sisters did about themselves and their accomplishments.

We owe it to our children to try to give them what

they need most: love and respect for their individuality. It is detrimental for parents to impose our own goals on children (possibly stemming from our own unfilled expectations of ourselves) or want them to excel in order to elevate our own status. We should want them to succeed in life according to how *they* define success — and accept that their perception might be quite different from ours.

Many parents mean well and act out of their best intentions and yet psychologically cripple their children because they insist on their own views and ideas, without allowing children to develop ideas of their own. Khalil Gibran's poem "On Children" expresses this notion beautifully:

> You may house their bodies but not their souls;
> For their souls dwell in the house of tomorrow,
> which you cannot visit, not even in your dreams.[7]

Our influence on our children's ability to form and maintain meaningful and loving relationships is tremendous, as a number of research studies have confirmed. For the famous Minnesota Twin Family Study, researchers evaluated more than one hundred sets of twins separated during early childhood to assess the influence of hereditary and environmental factors on personality. The investigators established that approximately 70 percent of our intelligence — as assessed by standard testing — is genetically determined.[8] For other psychological traits, such as personal interests and adherence to religion, the results also suggest considerable genetic disposition.

The researchers also studied twins in an effort to disentangle hereditary and environmental factors that influence dating behaviors.[9] For example, participants were asked to characterize their dating experiences with terms such as *passionate, game playing, friendship, practical, possessive,* or *altruistic.* Given the results from the Minnesota Twin Family Study as well as other research on personality traits showing high heritability, the investigators were surprised to find little evidence that innate factors influenced the participants' responses. These results suggest that in contrast to other personal characteristics, our patterns in conducting romantic relationships are largely the result of our upbringing and not something we were born with.

The finding of this research supports our concept of love as an art. While we have little influence over whether our children will become rocket scientists or movie stars, we have an enormous effect on their ability to attain happiness and maintain relationships in adulthood.[10]

9. Love and Religion

Can we separate love from religion? This question has occupied theologians and philosophers for centuries. Ultimately, the answer depends on our thoughts about our origin. If we believe that we were created by God — whatever our understanding of God may be — then we see love as a divine gift. If we do not, we may interpret love as an important biological drive. It is not helpful to compare the support for these views or attempt to discredit either one. People find comfort in both, and no one should be judged for their spiritual beliefs.

From a practical standpoint, with or without the underpinning of religion, love requires focus and devotion. We are all born with a capacity to love. This capacity likely varies in each person, but it is inherent in all. We are also born with numerous impulses that conflict with love. We need to learn to control these competing drives in order to sustain and express love.

The major world religions are remarkably consistent in their insistence on the need for devotion and effort in the quest for love and spiritual enlightenment. They all offer strikingly similar teachings on love, emphasizing that the defeat of egotism and the development of altruism are key for finding spiritual enlightenment and/or the path to God. All major religions recognize the necessity of a strong mental focus to suppress selfish impulses we inevitably experience. Jesus's command to love our enemies requires that we make enormous efforts to love. Developing such a great capacity to love would grant us happiness regardless of our circumstances. The Buddha emphasizes that defeating self-serving impulses, through rigorous meditation and deliberation, is essential to achieving inner peace. Reaching the state of nirvana implies a state of total selflessness, leading to dissolution of the self and oneness with all living things.[1]

The fact that the principle of selflessness is common, and fundamental, to all of the major world religions suggests that it strikes a central chord in the human mind. The Indian poet Rabindranath Tagore referred to love as the ultimate truth that lies at the heart of creation. In Hinduism, the most commonly pursued path to liberation of the soul is through love, in the form of total devotion to God. Similarly, in Judaism, Christianity, and Islam, the love of God is central to faith, with salvation and heaven being the reward for a life dedicated to God.

Although different religions frame their spiritual goals in different terms, they refer to the same underlying phenomenon: the state of inner harmony and satisfaction that comes from freeing ourselves from all self-directed impulses and gladly devoting ourselves to the happiness and well-being of others — that is, to love. Thus, a plausible explanation for the influence of the world's great spiritual leaders is that they recognized the power of love as the key to joyful human existence.

These religions all teach us that a state of peace can be attained by *anybody*, as long as we are willing to devote sufficient effort to it. As with love, attaining this state requires us to control competing impulses such as egocentric feelings, aggression, ambition, and lust, and religious teachings provide guidance on how best to resist these temptations. Because achieving complete control of our egotism is difficult, few succeed in following a perfect path, just as few become masters of the art of love.

Religions may emphasize love because love is the key to a happy, fulfilled life. The claim that love is a supernatural or God-given power is as valid as the argument that it is a biological drive to preserve the species. Regardless of the diversity of spiritual beliefs, love has been a powerful force throughout human history. We have learned that following the loving impulse predictably leads to processes in the human brain that induce contentment in the individual while reinforcing the species-serving action or thought. It is conceivable that because of the magnitude of the species-supporting benefit of loving, the intrinsic neurological reward for our focus on loving behavior is more enduring than that of other impulses. Accordingly, engaging in loving activities leads to the most lasting contentment among human activities and pursuits. While the internal reward — the release of euphoria-inducing hormones — in response to self-serving impulses may also be high, it is short-lived and ultimately less satisfying than the reward for following the impulse of love. Given the importance of preserving the species, we are true to our biological destiny if we control self-serving impulses and prioritize love.

It is easy to understand why love is often seen as a divine attribute and why religions place such importance on it. Love has a profound effect on how we perceive our lives and our environment. A focus on love can turn a feeling of misery into happiness — which may be viewed as miraculous. The serenity that arises from a loving mind may be felt as supernatural, particularly in the absence of other plausible explanations.

In addition to teaching love, religion has fulfilled many other functions over the centuries. Sigmund Freud believed that religions were human inventions created to satisfy certain needs, particularly to assist in dealing with the unbearable thought of mortality. Historically, religions have provided a framework for explaining otherwise baffling natural phenomena (a role that has diminished with the growth of scientific knowledge) and standards for ethical behavior among groups and populations. These rules are fundamental to cooperative human cohabitation.

The structure and core teachings of major religions

still provide enormous comfort and guidance to many people. They provide answers to questions that haunt human consciousness: Why are we here? What is our purpose in life? Their answer, in general, is that we should devote our lives to God. They encourage us to overcome selfishness, greed, envy, and other negative impulses while dedicating ourselves to achieving spiritual enlightenment.

Ironically, separating the concept of love from religion may allow for overcoming the greatest limitation of religion: divisiveness. While the goal of most religions is to unite people, it has often had the opposite effect. Once formed, religions (like any other social institution) develop dynamics shaped by the desire for power and influence, which are usually contrary to the original precepts of the religion.[2] Furthermore, the development of a group, by definition, involves distinguishing that group from other groups. Bitter conflicts and wars have resulted from religious differences.

The problem does not lie with the religious concepts, which are typically good. But while many people fail to follow the central teachings of their religion, such as "Love your neighbor," they may still maintain a disdainful, exclusionary, or hostile attitude to those with other spiritual beliefs.

In a world that is increasingly driven by logic and science, it is becoming more difficult for many to subscribe to religious explanations of our existence. For this and other reasons, the influence of organized religions has been declining. A worldwide survey found a 9 percent decrease in respondents claiming to be religious between 2005 and 2012 (and a 13 percent decrease in the United States).[3] The same survey revealed that nonreligious people and atheists are the majority in China, Japan, and several Western European countries. However, science cannot provide an easy answer to the deep-seated question, "What is our purpose in life?"

Largely for this reason, established religions still attract many people. Yet even without the trappings of religion, love itself can help us identify our reason for living. The loving person finds meaning and purpose in life by creating happiness for others. If someone has a better, happier life because of us, then our life is meaningful. We cannot heal the whole world, but by helping individuals, we can do our part. If we live a life respecting, helping, and loving others, the world is indeed a better place because of us.

Dedicating our lives to love thus creates meaning of the highest kind — whether or not we do it within the framework of religion. Giving love creates fulfillment and happiness in the giver because it responds to humans' most powerful intrinsically determined impulse. Love even provides an answer to our fear of mortality. Our love does not die. It lives on in all beings who are touched by that love. Most of us still feel loved by certain people even though they have passed away. Remembering their actions and words brings back the feelings of love. We not only remember the emotion, but we pass it on to others by emulating the loved ones' actions or words.

Love itself, therefore, may be regarded as a religion, or a spiritual path, in the sense that it provides answers to life's most essential questions. While love is the common denominator and the core of the major traditional religions, the advantage of regarding love itself as a religion is that it is truly universal and applicable to all humans. Love is never exclusionary. Indeed, the religion of love has existed for thousands of years. Those who believe in it and follow its rules form a community independent of borders, cultures, and languages. If you meet a truly loving person, you feel an immediate bond, no matter where you are, even if you speak a different language and have never seen this person before. The community of love is the largest in the world.

The religion of love has no specific rituals and customs. This may be a disadvantage in some ways, because such traditions, like other cultural habits, provide a sense of familiarity, community, and comfort. For individuals who seek the comforts of such practices and a local community for sharing beliefs, some religious faiths and denominations, such as the Unitarian Universalists, attempt to combine the teaching of love with traditional religious observances from various faiths. For others, the strength and courage they gather from the art of loving, outside any religious structure or institution, may be all they need.

"I care not for a man's religion whose dog and cat are not the better for it" is a saying often attributed to Abraham Lincoln. What matters most is how we conduct ourselves, irrespective of our spiritual or philosophical beliefs. If we claim to be pious but judge others by their spiritual beliefs, we are poor representatives of our creed. If we accept others as they are and practice kindness to everybody, we reflect the good and loving in human existence. A verse from the New Testament, "Let us love not in word and speech, but in action and truth" (1 John 3:18), is frequently quoted, but how often is it truly applied?

10. Love and Society

What role does love play in society? What role should it play? The word *society* comes from the Latin word *socius*, meaning "friend" or "ally." A society describes a union among people for the purpose of peaceful living. Within this framework, however, people have different views about the desired relationship among a society's members, which may range from loving to merely being civil. Conflicts between selfish and loving impulses observed in an individual are magnified in a society. For the good of the community, members may be asked to relinquish possessions (for example, by paying taxes), provide services, and surrender some of their freedom to act. The extent of these sacrifices is often a point of contention. Furthermore, envy and greed among members have caused tension and struggles in human societies.

Ideally, members of a society have a strong sense of community and work toward the happiness and well-being of all. Society offers the important advantage of being able to use shared resources to provide support to ill, disabled, or other less fortunate members. By carefully allocating its resources, a society may avoid wealth inequality, which is a major cause of conflict.

Fromm argued in the 1950s that Western industrial society is not conducive to love. Capitalism promotes competition and originality as well as hard work to outdo competitors. Western society is built on consumption, and thus it supports activities that increase consumption. Advertising encouraging us to buy more surrounds us in the form of junk mail, billboards, radio, television, newspapers, magazines, and now the internet. Social status is largely based on material wealth.

Competition for status begins early in elementary school. Children with the more expensive electronic equipment, fancier clothes, and other trendy gadgets gain respect and envy. Later in school, students compete fiercely for grades to facilitate access to the best universities and graduate schools, which in turn increases their chances for a successful and lucrative career. Many people now spend most of the first three decades of their lives studying and training for careers.

With so much focus on career, there is little time to devote to personal development. School and early career are followed by busy years of parenting and work. It is not surprising that many of us face a crisis in our thirties and forties. Eventually, we awaken from our autopilot career-and-family mode and wonder whether we have really made the choices that were best for us, or whether we were just trying to meet parental or social expectations. Many of us do not figure out what we really want from life until much later — and some never find out. Other cultures and religions recognize some confusion about personal goals as a normal part of maturing. However, we can never retrieve the many years we may have spent with a potentially misdirected focus in life.

The pressure to consume and to be able to consume diverts important energy away from introspection and learning to know ourselves. Understanding our nature is almost antithetical to functioning in a society centered on commerce. An unfulfilled individual is more likely to consume in order to alleviate feelings of loneliness or lack of self-worth. Conversely, happy and loving people typically are content with fewer possessions and enjoy nonmaterial pleasures, such as the company of family and friends and the beauties of nature.[1]

In a market-driven culture, love is a product, albeit an important one. Because most people long for love and sex, products associated with love and sex tend to sell well. And because physical attractiveness is widely perceived as improving a person's chances of finding love and sex, companies take in billions of dollars each year selling cosmetics, perfumes, hair and skin treatments, clothes, jewelry, weight-loss and body-building products, surgery, and more. Movies, magazines, books, computer games, and other media dealing with love and sex sell well. In fact, associating almost any product with love or sex is likely to increase sales.[2]

The portrayal of love in the media underscores this quest to purchase love and sex. In movies and magazines, romantic love happens preferentially to beautiful people. The message is that if you are beautiful (by conventional standards), you don't need to look for love — love will find *you*. This message tells people that they should focus on physical attractiveness rather than on personal development and effort. Since it is appealing to believe that love will simply find us, given the right conditions, producers promise us that their consumer goods will foster these conditions. The perception of love as requiring dedication, introspection, and discipline is a much less attractive vision and hardly conducive to promoting sales.

Of course, there is nothing wrong with consumption per se. Our economic system has provided us with abundant amenities, comforts, and health benefits. The problem arises when consumption comes at the expense of self-development and love. Life is about balance. Uncontrolled markets are unkind: they show no concern for those left behind and in need. Communism, at the other end of the spectrum, aims to be kind but neglects the human drive for ingenuity as well as the beneficial aspects of competitiveness. As so often, the answer lies in the middle.

Different societies prioritize different values, such as education, wisdom, and seniority. To change our society's values, we would need to rebalance society altogether, placing less emphasis on consumption and more on the recognition and practice of love. This vision is not

as impractical as it may appear. There is a growing awareness of the contentment arising from compassion rather
than self-centeredness, which becomes apparent when we
look back just a hundred years. In the United States of the
early twentieth century, women had no or limited voting
rights, racial segregation was widespread, and homosex-
uality was a crime. Our achievements in civil rights are a
reflection of our society's desire for fairness and compassion for others. While there is a lot of work left to do, we
have come a long way over the course of a few decades.
Progress often occurs in waves, intermittently meeting
resistance and slowing. Based on the evolutionary principles outlined earlier, however, we can be optimistic about
the further development of love in human societies.

In the interim, an individual striving for personal
development must make a conscious effort to resist consumer pressures. Intermittently, most of us realize that we
focus way too much on things that should not matter, and
we try to adjust our attitude. During the holiday season,
we declare, along with George Bailey (played by James
Stewart) in the movie *It's a Wonderful Life,* that as long
as we have friends and family, nothing else really matters.
However, a few weeks into the New Year, most of us are
back to our routines, and all of our resolutions to spend
more time on the really important things are gone. The
challenge is to maintain our focus on love at *all* times.

We choose what is most important to us at any given
moment. We always have the option to choose love —
but we often don't. Our obsession with commerce clearly

affects our ability to develop love and relationships. It takes maturity and love to be able to recognize this impulse, but, ironically, because maturity and love are unlikely to develop when we devote most of our energy to earning and spending money, this insight may never occur. Instead, our fixation on societal status and material values may create a vicious cycle. Envy for other people's wealth may corrupt our thinking, in the extreme case even leading to theft and other crimes.

It is often monumental events that cause us to stop and reflect on what leads to true happiness. Some millionaires who lost everything in the 2008 financial crisis reported that they were ultimately happier than they were before because their monetary loss made them refocus on the truly important things in life. Others have similar moments of insight when they face a serious illness or even death.

Why does it take a catastrophe to make us understand that we should strive for balance in our lives and that we need to devote time to ourselves and our loved ones to live happily? We are social but also competitive creatures. The attraction to power is a strong inherent impulse. If social status is based on money and material possessions, we are motivated to strive for those things. Love, on the other hand, requires rejection of competing, egotistic drives, such as ambition. The result is an obvious conflict.

Today we face increasing distractions from love as the result of technological advancement. Many of us spend more time with electronic devices than with other people. Digital communication has taken over large portions of our peer-to-peer interactions. The pervasiveness of social media now often requires children to start negotiating group dynamics and competition at a young age. Electronic devices, the main form of entertainment in Western societies, leave us less time and energy to focus on love. Virtual reality devices, which are growing in capacity and popularity, represent yet another means of removing ourselves from interpersonal contact and the natural world.

Resisting society's many pressures requires awareness, which goes hand in hand with focus. Aristotle, like many other philosophers and spiritual leaders, saw the value of life as dependent on awareness and the power of contemplation. The Buddha emphasized constant awareness to detect selfishness, which is the root of suffering. Constant striving for awareness of our environment leads to realization and critical reflection on our actions and thoughts.

Let's look at a trivial example: I am shopping for new clothes. I may ask myself: "Why am I shopping for new clothes? Do I need them to keep me warm, or am I buying clothes to make myself more interesting? Why do I need to make myself more interesting? What might be my subconscious impulse? Should this be a priority?" Questions like these may reveal our motives to ourselves and help us be true to ourselves rather than giving in to the pressures of a materialistic society.

The opposite of awareness is ignorance — the enemy of love. Unfortunately, we spend most of our time in ignorance, too absorbed in the demands of our daily lives to see the larger picture. Ironically, it is often bankruptcy, illness, or other major challenges that allow us to finally recognize what really matters.

For the most part, we do not confront existential questions every day; instead we focus on day-to-day necessities. However, appreciating the gift of every day is precisely what helps us to enjoy life to the fullest. Every single moment, we have the opportunity to focus on our good fortune in sharing this incredible experience called life.

11. Love and the World

The loving mind recognizes the value and beauty in every living thing. It seeks to preserve and protect the world around us, including our environment. A loving person is incapable of committing acts of violence, betrayal, theft, or other social or ethical crimes, or of exploiting other humans, animals, and natural resources out of greed and selfishness. The loving individual suffers with any destruction but rejoices at every act of kindness.

World affairs are often managed by politicians and businesspeople whose prevailing impulses are not loving. Politics and economic wealth appeal to a very strong human impulse, the drive for power. The philosopher Friedrich Nietzsche coined the term *Wille zur Macht* (will to power) to describe what he regarded as a central human drive to reach the highest attainable position in a group.[1] Nietzsche believed the will to power to be the main force underlying human behavior.

From an evolutionary standpoint, it is intuitive that the drive for power should be a strong impulse, because a dominant position in a group allows a greater probability of successful reproduction — both in terms of the number of progeny and the probability that offspring will survive to reproductive age. A powerful person can provide for more sexual partners and more children.[2] He or she also is better positioned to protect himself or herself from antagonists and to support descendants. Accordingly, striving for power, wealth, and comfort is a strong trait in humans, one that frequently trumps considerations of love in political and business decisions.

Following the will to power requires self-serving impulses to prevail, and these often conflict with impulses to serve others. Even for those who manage to reach a position of power without compromising their integrity, the desire to remain in power may clash strongly with their intentions to control egotistic impulses. The disastrous result for world affairs — and for humanity — is that people who obtain commanding positions are often not driven by a focus on loving.

Conversely, those who prioritize love in their lives are less likely to end up in highly influential roles. They are more likely to focus on family, community, and volunteer work. Furthermore, people who immerse themselves in loving activities are often indifferent to politics, leaving contests for political leadership open to those who are hungry for power. These dynamics pave the way for governments and important institutions to be headed by egomaniacs driven by the desire for influence and control instead of a genuine aspiration to improve people's lives. The renowned psychologist Carl G. Jung summarized this pattern: "Where love rules, there is no will to power; and where power predominates, there love is lacking. The one is the shadow of the other."[3] Occasionally, we see world leaders who retain a strong focus on loving after rising to positions of great influence. Sadly, these individuals remain exceptional.

The economic and political impact of the lack of love in world affairs is difficult to ascertain with any precision, but it is surely enormous. International politics is fundamentally not different from interactions between individuals. A nation devoted exclusively to advancing its own interests, without any concern for its global neighbors, will earn resentment and opposition from other nations rather than cooperation and goodwill.

Political leadership that is not guided by love is also likely to foster inequality, hardship, and injustice, which in turn may lead to violent conflict. Research suggests that the perception of injustice is among the most important motivations for terrorism.[4] If a country's polices are perceived by others as threatening their fundamental rights, such as the freedom of religion, they may elicit fervent and violent resistance.

On the other hand, as in interpersonal dealings, if a government's policies and actions demonstrate care and respect for others, it gains credibility and trust and undermines support for antagonizing, extreme voices. The same applies to citizens who live under an unjust and immoral government. The genuinely caring policies of another nation may weaken the authority of the corrupt government, whereas confrontation and threat only unify opponents and escalate conflict.[5] Importantly, compassionate politics facilitate the building of broad alliances to isolate nations that violate human rights.

Like love, amicable relationships between nations require effort and introspection. If a nation's leaders do not try to understand the effect of the nation's actions on others, it will be difficult to have good international relationships. If they make errors of judgment and antagonize other nations (or factions within nations), they must concentrate on restoring others' trust by acknowledging their mistakes and by displaying consistently honorable behavior. While such an approach will not convince all extremists to drop their weapons, it will erode the support for extremists and discourage followers from joining an antagonistic group, which is a critical measure for containing extremist movements.

Many believe, however, that international leadership requires a show of strength and that it is naive and dangerous to trust in the goodwill of others.[6] Ultimately, it comes down to our view of human beings. Do we believe people are inherently selfish, greedy, and hostile, or that people generally act from good intentions but may sometimes be misguided?

The former attitude has led to worldwide distrust and suspicion, hampering progress in international relationships.[7] An approach of respect and goodwill is more likely to bring peace and cooperation in the long term. Along with numerous devastating wars, world history contains many examples of treaties and agreements between nations. At the heart of diplomacy is the willingness to compromise: to respect another party's interests and to make concessions. Leaders with a genuine interest in peace and in improving the human condition will choose this path whenever possible.

Before World War I, for instance, the nineteenth-century Prussian statesman Otto von Bismarck carefully arranged a balance of power among European nations by crafting a number of alliances. Bismarck is credited with preserving the peace during turbulent times in Europe, as many countries strove for power and influence.

Little more than a decade after Bismarck, however, Europe was careering toward war. World War I — which the American diplomat and historian George F. Kennan called the "seminal catastrophe" of the twentieth century, and which paved the way for World War II — is now widely regarded as resulting from failures of leadership and diplomacy.[8] Considerate actions by European leaders could plausibly have prevented the seventeen million deaths as well as the destruction that ravaged the continent. Winston Churchill believed, as many historians do today, that World War II and its sixty million deaths could have been prevented if the international community had worked together to contain Hitler.[9]

The fundamental principle of love applies to all human interactions, from the individual to the global scale. It helps to remember that this planet is our home and that we are all related: we have much more uniting us than separating us. Most people indeed are well-meaning and want to live peacefully: avoiding conflict is an evolutionary impulse that promotes survival.

Does this mean all people are good? Certainly many people all over the world display disrespectful, selfish, greedy behavior at times. We may not be able to change their ways, but we can control our own actions and form alliances among those with common interests. Leading with integrity has always inspired others because it speaks to our strongest intrinsic, evolutionary purpose: that is, to unite our species for the sake of its survival rather than to divide it.

It is evident that the human impact on our planet has been disastrous. We are flooding the earth with our waste and pollutants, destroying other species with whom we share it. We were given a paradise, but we seem to be doing our best to turn it into hell. It is easy to assign blame, but it is difficult for individuals to halt the destruction in which we are all, to some degree, complicit.

The first step toward effecting change is awareness and recognition of what we are doing to the world. Love requires us to value other lives. We cannot expect love for ourselves while being unloving to others. Loving involves respecting and nurturing life, recognizing the miracle in every being. To have love in our lives requires us to love the world. Exploitation of other humans, animals, or our environment may lead to material gain, but it will preclude our own happiness.

12. Love and Human Differences

Humans are mostly alike, yet we often perceive ourselves as very different from others. Such perceptions of difference may create obstacles to love. It is easy for us to love some people, particularly our children and those who love us. The more affection we receive from somebody, the easier it is to love that person. But, as Jesus asked, "If you love those who love you, what credit is that to you? For even sinners love those who love them" (Luke 6:32).

It is also often easy for us to love those with whom we have a lot in common and to regard them as members of our social group. The urge to be part of a group is a powerful human impulse. Group membership offers individuals strength, importance, and, potentially, status.[1] Particularly for people who have trouble with their self-esteem, these are attractive attributes, and we feel loyalty and sometimes strong affection for the members of the group that provides us with them. People outside the group, however, may be regarded as different, not necessarily worthy of love.

Who does or does not belong to a group, of course, is largely a matter of perspective. For example, if people from two different American towns support opposing football teams, each may be quite hostile toward fans of the other team. However, the same people are likely to welcome each other when meeting accidentally in another country. They identify as Americans, not supporters of rival teams. From that perspective, they may even see their antagonism over football team loyalties as silly. The perceived commonality — their common nationality — may prevail over differences.

Nationality can be a powerful form of group identity. Although it is often marked by positive feelings of loyalty and altruism toward the nation and fellow citizens, it also may entail arrogance and animosity toward members of other countries. Such a worldview often leads us to forget that we are all living on the same planet: we are one big family. More than two thousand years ago, Diogenes of Sinope, when asked where he was from, responded: "I am a citizen of the world."[2] If more of us could adopt this view, the world would contain far less hostility.

There is nothing wrong with being proud of our local team, our town, or our country. Claiming membership in any of these groups can bring us confidence and joy. However, healthy patriotism knows its limits: it accepts the integration of smaller groups into the larger community.

The insanity of humans' territorial behavior may be illustrated by imagining extraterrestrials approaching the Earth. After visiting many galaxies during years of travel, they reach ours and see a miraculously blue, shimmering world. As they get closer, they can't believe the immense beauty they see: water everywhere, colorful plants, food hanging from trees and bushes, animals in all forms and shapes, magnificent landscapes. Truly, this looks like the closest thing to paradise.

Then they discover that humans are in control of this world. To the extraterrestrials' astonishment, the humans, instead of enjoying the endless pleasures their world provides, have divided the planet into territories called countries, and they fight and kill each other for control of these territories. The humans in one country disdain the humans in the other, although there is no difference between them except arbitrary lines on a map. They worship different gods, and each group claims to worship the true one. They exploit plants and animals. They poison the water and land they depend on. The extraterrestrials must conclude that these earthlings are the most foolish and most undeserving creatures imaginable: they share a paradise of unbelievable beauty but do much to spoil it.

To improve our world, it helps to remember that the differences between people are small and unimportant, and to think of other people as fellow human beings and not as members of a particular country, race, religion, or any other group. Such differences are simply our perceptions: they exist only in our minds, as a result of our upbringing and environment. As we do when we love, we must make a continuous effort for benevolence when thinking of others, and by doing so we may recognize the absurdity of viewing people across the world as foreign or different. While humans undoubtedly face challenges regarding living space and resources, our chance of success increases with a common strategy.

Many would agree in principle that we should be accepting and respectful of others — until we start talking about citizens of a "hostile" country. Right away, we may begin to generalize about the character and value of everyone living there. To avoid slipping into stereotyping and bigotry, it helps if we try hard to see things through the eyes of others. Stepping back may allow us to see the same situation from a broader perspective and change our attitude. There is no such thing as a country full of bad people. Countries may be governed by individuals hostile to others, but their inhabitants, like everybody else, generally want to live a peaceful life.

Acceptance of others is of paramount importance today. Many Western countries are seeing rising numbers of immigrants from Asia, Africa, and the Middle East, while people of European ancestry are likely soon to become minorities in the United States and Western Europe. This diversity holds great potential for social and economic growth, as people from different backgrounds bring new perspectives. Research in economy, sociology, psychology, and epidemiology shows that socially diverse groups are more innovative than homogeneous groups.[3]

Exposure to social diversity in childhood and adolescence is associated with greater academic development.

Social diversity also leads to the cultural enrichment of a society. The most obvious example is the introduction of new cuisines with the arrival of immigrants. It is difficult to imagine Western cuisine today without the influences of Chinese, Indian, Japanese, Mexican, Middle Eastern, and other cuisines.

Even so, many people are skeptical of the benefits of diversity and are openly hostile toward immigrants. This is particularly tragic when those people have not simply chosen to migrate in search of a better life but are desperately fleeing war, oppression, or other kinds of disaster. Some people in the receiving country may view them with suspicion and hostility because a small number of their compatriots are malicious. Yet the same is equally true of the people we mix with every day, or those in the next city over. Should fear of some small risk stop us from doing the right thing and extending a welcome to immigrants and refugees?

There is a small town in Germany called Lüchow, home to about seven thousand people.[4] It is a typical German town: quaint, with many half-timbered houses, a picturesque setting, and pretty churches. In the summer of 2015, the government established a camp for 550 refugees there almost overnight. Very quickly, the number grew to more than 700 refugees — a tenth of the town's population. Most of the refugees were from Syria or Iraq. They included many families with children. It is easy to imagine that the town's inhabitants would have been uneasy about the sudden and large influx of foreigners from different cultures and religions who didn't speak German.

While Germany's acceptance of hundreds of thousands of refugees led to large-scale protests elsewhere, this little town took a different approach. From day one, it warmly welcomed the refugees. Lüchow's people crowded the streets not in protest but to stand in line to offer help. Indeed, the only complaints the local government received from residents were that their ideas for supporting the refugees were not sufficiently acknowledged. The day the first refugees arrived, townspeople brought flowers and sang songs. People started projects to offer financial support, integrate the refugees into the town's social and educational activities, and assist the refugees in establishing stores and other businesses. Schoolchildren invited refugee teenagers to join their soccer teams and taught them how to skate. Social media is being used to organize integration and to foster ideas to ease the refugees' transition to their new lives.

People in Lüchow respect the refugees' cultural and religious differences. They have helped organize celebrations for Islamic holidays and offered gifts and food. The refugees have tried to reciprocate the kindness they have experienced by doing their best to support their new community.

The people of Lüchow could have given in to impulses of fear of the changes in their community or resentment of the newcomers. However, they chose to reject these concerns and focused on a loving attitude to their fellow human beings. They did not view the refugees as intruders: they saw people in need and opened their arms. As a result, they enriched their own lives as much as those of their new neighbors.

Do some refugees betray their receiving country and commit acts of violence? Yes — just as some native citizens do. Despite the distress and financial hardship that refugees may experience, crime statistics do not support the notion that refugees are more violent than natives.[5] Research does, however, suggest that people may become antagonistic and even radicalized if they are marginalized by society.[6] The example of Lüchow suggests such a risk to be low if we aim for integration rather than exclusion in a community.

13. Love and Happiness

Most people would agree that attaining happiness is an important goal. But what is happiness? Like love, happiness is not clearly defined, and it means different things in different contexts. Generally, happiness in life refers not just to transient episodes of joy but rather to how fully our expectations of life have been met. Happiness depends on the individual's mindset and our perception of self-worth. Some people are very content, while others are miserable despite similar conditions: some see the glass as half full, others as half empty. How we identify our expectations from life, therefore, is critical for achieving fulfillment.[1]

Is our perception of happiness influenced by our genes? Recent genetic research involving several hundred thousand individuals in many countries indeed found genes associated with greater life satisfaction and other genes linked to depression or neuroticism.[2] This, of course, does not mean that our happiness depends

entirely on our genes. As with many genetic predispositions, it means that different people may find it innately
easier or harder to be happy, but our emotional outlook is
strongly influenced by our environment and our own effort. A naturally gifted sprinter may seem a better candi-
date to win a race than someone with less favorable body
characteristics, but the latter may compensate with more
training and greater effort.

In *The Conquest of Happiness*, Bertrand Russell ex-
plores patterns of unhappiness and examples of people who achieved happiness in life. Russell identifies as
sources of unhappiness attitudes and endeavors that
reflect conflicts between the self and the world, such as
envy and a thirst for power or reputation, as well as in-
difference to the external world.[3] Conversely, he views
integration with the world as the principal way to achieve
happiness in life.

What does integration with the world mean? It implies the fusion of an individual's interests with those of
others to the extent that they are indistinguishable. A
person's internal world is not separate from the external
world but rather part of a continual stream of life. Integration eliminates concerns for the self and also the fear
of death, because other lives, past, present, and future,
are part of one's own life, and vice versa. This view re-
sembles the Buddhist state of nirvana or the union with
God that is the goal of many religions. Russell's view is
another endorsement of selflessness and love as the root
of contentment and liberation.

These goals are worth striving for but are fully achieved by only a few. The psychologist Carl Jung identified more concrete elements of happiness: good physical and mental health, good personal and intimate relationships, the faculty for perceiving beauty in art and nature, a reasonable standard of living, satisfactory work, and a philosophical or religious point of view capable of coping with the vicissitudes of life.[4]

Jung's advice provides more practical guidance for a contemporary society. While a life devoted to selflessness brings bliss, it may be more realistic for most of us to integrate our efforts toward love and selflessness with the pursuit of happiness from a number of different sources. Because happiness is more easily achieved in the absence of worries, maintaining good health, adequate living standards, and financial security may help keep our focus on relationships and love.

Creativity — explored through art and craft — is a source of happiness. Fromm argued that the satisfaction we derive from creativity comes from our sense of union with our creation, giving us a sense of continuity as well as the satisfaction of contributing to our community. Creativity, therefore, shares some of the elements of love, which may explain some of the fulfillment that it brings us.

The underlying principles of Jung's recipe for happiness are very much consistent with Russell's paradigm of integration: focusing on relationships, appreciation for our environment, and respectful interaction with the world. The force behind these elements is love.

Even in the face of adversity, we can alleviate pain with the right focus and attitude. My friend Kerstin has a fine sense for "doing the right thing" and is always there for others. Born with a positive, cheerful attitude, Kerstin is a good person to have around. Even so, her care and consideration for others often have not been reciprocated. She has found friends, but her search for a life partner has been filled with bitter disappointments. In her thirties she sustained an illness that put an end to her hopes for having children.

Kerstin's professional life has also been full of setbacks. She earned a degree for a very competitive profession and spent years working in a low-skill labor market, waiting for a chance to pursue her desired career. In her mid-forties, she still lives with her mother and works in retail, albeit with a freelance engagement on the side.

By the standards of our society, Kerstin's life has been filled with disappointments. Kerstin has been loving and kind all her life, but that does not seem to have helped her to live a happy, fulfilled life. Or has it? Kerstin is happy because she focuses on her good fortune rather than her misfortunes. She cherishes her love for her parents, her brother, and friends. She travels the world and enjoys the wonder of life in different cultures and other places.

There is no absolute criterion for success: it depends solely on our own values and perceptions. The more we are able to free ourselves from outside standards, the easier it is to find contentment. If we value our lives by external benchmarks and then fail to meet them, we set ourselves up for frustration and disappointment.

It is possible that Kerstin has had to work harder at maintaining a loving attitude than people who have been luckier in life, according to our society's standards. She has managed to achieve happiness by focusing on the many beautiful things in her life. Despite her bad luck with her job and relationships, she chose optimism instead of despair.

Distraction is a major challenge to cherishing life. Our days are so packed with obligations and routine activities that we often don't find the time to reflect on and appreciate the beauty of our existence. It helps to try to step back and look at our lives from a distance. We may see it as ludicrous that we allow our preoccupation with duties and commitments to stop us from appreciating the good fortune of being alive.

14. Love and Health

Love not only helps us live more happily but also helps us live longer. Happy marriages are associated with better health, while tension in relationships increases stress and the risk of illness.[1] An analysis of studies involving hundreds of thousands of people suggests that maintaining good social relationships is associated with lower mortality.[2] Conversely, social isolation ranks among the most significant physical and lifestyle risk factors for mortality, such as diabetes, high blood pressure, and cigarette smoking.

This association does not prove causality: we can't tell whether the boost to longevity comes from the relationship itself or from other factors associated with a relationship. For example, it is conceivable that being married contributes to better health by encouraging better diet or hygiene. It is also possible that healthier people or those with fewer unhealthy habits, such as drug or alcohol abuse, may be more likely to get married in the first place, thus skewing the analysis. Yet studies that controlled for these factors have shown similar results for lower mortality in happily married people.[3]

On the other hand, *unhappiness* is associated with many types of organ dysfunction and disease. Even brief angry outbursts have now been linked to an increased risk of heart attacks.[4] One study of immunity among socially isolated people showed that they had poorer immune function and greater stress levels than those with many social contacts.[5]

In the extreme case, stress can lead to health crises. We have recently learned that acute emotional stress can lead to actual heart failure — a serious illness known as *broken heart syndrome*, which is now regularly identified in medical centers around the world.[6] While the exact mechanisms leading to weakening of the heart muscle remain unclear, we know that high levels of certain stress hormones, which are released in response to a devastating breakup or personal loss, or extreme fear or anxiety, may trigger the syndrome. Fortunately, many patients recover after a few weeks.

A large body of evidence suggests that love has a direct effect on a vast array of biological functions.[7] A loving relationship fosters the release of the hormone oxytocin, the "love hormone." Oxytocin has a variety of purposes and is probably best known for its release after childbirth to foster bonding between mother and baby. Oxytocin is also implicated in attachment during relationships and many other human interactions. It has antidepressive effects that are being investigated for clinical use. Of particular interest is the discovery that oxytocin may decrease the levels of the hormone cortisol.[8] Changes in cortisol levels are associated with sleep deprivation and physical and emotional stress, and cortisol has a well-known weakening effect on our immune system. It may, therefore, not be surprising that happy relationships are associated with lower rates of sickness.

Good emotional health leads to good physical health.[9] And just as good physical health requires us to exercise, acquiring good emotional health also requires training. Emotional health "workouts" may include regular, conscious efforts to focus on love and relationships while deemphasizing material or career goals. As with physical exercise, it may take months or years of devoted practice to get into good emotional shape. This is because less healthy thinking patterns acquired early in life tend to be reinforced over years or even decades, making them difficult to reverse.

At any given moment we have the choice of allowing our thoughts and actions to be moved by impulses such as anger, frustration, jealousy, and boredom, or overcoming these impulses and acting out of love. If we choose love, we immediately feel a sensation of calm and peace, and things seem different. It works instantly and predictably. It is ironic that our society yearns for instant gratification and pursues various strategies for achieving instant wealth and fame — which essentially never work — while the immediate reward of a happy mind is instantly available to everybody but often not recognized.

Life is about balance. While we cannot control our genes or all the things that happen to us, we can help ourselves a lot by nurturing both our mind and our body and by placing a stronger emphasis on love. This undertaking requires focus and devotion, but the results are impressive. Devoting time to the art of love is a smart investment. Not only do we directly foster our own happiness, but we also support our health and chances of a longer, better life.

15. Love and the Meaning of Life

Distinguished from the animal world by the capacity of reason, humans have always thought about our place in the universe and beyond. Do we belong to nature, or are we above it? Are we a part of a greater plan or just a product of chance? What does existence really mean? Is there a meaning at all? While modern science has given us many answers about our origin, it has not brought us much closer to understanding our metaphysical being. We have made great strides in understanding our biology, but we still struggle to grasp our reason for existing.

Philosophers, religious scholars, and creative artists have wrestled with this question throughout human history. Although their conclusions vary widely, one element is remarkably consistent: the belief that human suffering is relieved by achieving a state of *selflessness*, sometimes referred to as a "liberation of the soul." We achieve peace by defeating our instinct for egotism.

Again, one explanation for this phenomenon may lie in evolutionary biology and psychology. Since an impulse for maintaining the well-being of the species ranks higher than one directed at aiding only the individual, the reinforcing feedback from the former will be greater and more sustained. Thus, all attempts to grasp the purpose of our existence — including the construction of elaborate intellectual or spiritual schemes — are challenged by the somewhat bleak-sounding argument that we are here merely to perpetuate our species.

Even if this is the case, if we adhere to our biological programming by practicing benevolence toward others, we will live in harmony with our bodies and perceive contentment. Conversely, self-serving actions — beyond caring for our own well-being — will bring us conflict and suffering. Even if we cannot explain the purpose of life itself, we may as well spend our given time closely aligned to the intrinsic intention of human nature.

Ultimately, we all have to determine for ourselves the meaning of life. For many, love has been the answer, and it has brought them happiness and contentment. Yet the truly loving person does not love pragmatically, with the aim of gaining happiness, but rather as a consequence of having matured into a complete person — or, in the words of the Buddha, "having awoken."

When we learn to contain impulses like greed and selfishness, love can develop freely, and we can experience the contentment and happiness that come from giving love. Parents know the overwhelming feeling of joy that comes from just looking at our children. They may cause us lots of work, sorrow, and hardship, but these are easily outweighed by the happiness we feel when we see the glee in our children's eyes and hear their laughter. Giving happiness to others is a great gift, and no amount of wealth or fame can match its satisfaction.[1]

Anyone can find purpose and meaning in life. Our success largely depends on how much effort and focus we are willing to expend. Love is not free — in the sense that it may require as much dedication and focus as any other great aim in life. The good news is that we can have it if we really want it and are willing to value it over other goals.

Identifying a purpose in life is closely linked to attaining happiness and fulfillment. Often, it is life events that prompt us to reflect on our purpose. In my case, it was the birth of my son Luca — or, strictly speaking, the time just before his birth. When my wife, Denise, was pregnant with Luca, we received notice that some of the routine prenatal tests showed results outside the normal range. Subsequent testing raised the possibility that Luca had trisomy-21, or Down syndrome. To have certainty and to be able to prepare for this possibility, we decided to have an amniocentesis. To discuss the results, we were invited for an appointment with the genetic counselor.

Coming to the appointment directly from work, I was a little late, and Denise and the counselor were talking when I entered the room. I will never forget the expressions on their faces when they looked at me, confirming the diagnosis. The counselor left the room to give Denise and me a minute to process the information. We hugged and were silent for a while. In hindsight and with shame, I remember a sensation of sadness and loss. My thoughts circled around not being able to share existential thoughts with my son, concepts that likely would be lost on him because of the intellectual disability associated with Down syndrome. I was afraid I would never have an intellectual connection to him.

It took me a while to realize that I was being selfish to worry about my unfulfilled expectations instead of asking what the diagnosis would mean for his life. Luca prompted me to think what life is all about. Is high intellectual capacity a prerequisite for a good life? Certainly not.

While there may not be a single criterion for the value of a life, it was important to me to know that Luca had the potential for experiencing happiness. Since his diagnosis was not associated with any impairment to receiving and giving love, and thus being able to live a happy life, my initial response of sadness was unjustified.

Because Denise arrived at the same conclusions way before I did, we were ready to welcome Luca into our lives with open arms. Since then, Luca has continued to teach us lessons of love. His sense for closeness among family and friends, his keen attention to the well-being of everybody around him, his astounding selflessness, and his amazing capacity for joy inspire us every day. My wife's description of Luca "oozing" love captures it best.

Luca may never win a Nobel Prize, but he exemplifies to us on a daily basis the happiness of life.

Trying to grasp the meaning of life is an overwhelming task, one that may trigger anxiety or denial. Central to such anxiety is facing our mortality, which is unbearable to many. Other than denial, there are many ways to deal with the fact of our mortality. Most of them entail a belief that we live on in one form or another. Christians, Jews, and Muslims believe that the soul moves on to a better world after death. Hinduism and Buddhism embrace the idea of reincarnation.

With the fading of religion, particularly in Western societies, and the simultaneous growth in influence of science and technology, people seek other ways to cope with finding meaning in life. It may be harder and more frightening, though, to seek the answers without the support of a spiritual community or organization. The struggle with finding life's meaning may be linked to the rising suicide rates among middle-aged adults in recent years.[2] Finding the answers for ourselves requires confidence to follow our own path.

Some people find reassurance about mortality in a quest for fame. This is based on the idea that we live on after death through our achievements, such as books, movies, music, and athletic achievements.

Probably the most common way to find meaning and to cope with our mortality is by having children. The strong bond we feel with our children is at least partly rooted in the idea that we live on in them, through their genes and their memories. As our children grow, we observe part of ourselves repeating the cycle of life, and we see it enacted again in our grandchildren. We recognize physical features and character traits in our children that resemble ours — or even our parents'. Witnessing the cycle of life is a comfort when we face our own individual mortality.

Love is a form of energy. A kind word or a thoughtful gesture — even exchanged with a stranger in a brief encounter — makes us feel warm and alive inside, ready to do something loving ourselves. When somebody dies, we still feel their love transmitting energy to us and steering us along the right path. When we die, our love and generosity will live on through the people we have known and loved. We can be comforted by the knowledge that we have been part of a positive force in this world.

Love thus offers a direct remedy for our fear of dying. The highest form of love is the achievement of selflessness and perfect union with the world around us. When we attain this state, our individual existence ceases to matter, as we perceive ourselves as part of the eternal stream of life. Another view of the same phenomenon is that a total focus on love — which is directed at others — eliminates any concerns for ourselves, including the fear of death.

Identifying our individual purpose is largely under our own control. In Western societies, success and purpose are commonly defined in terms of monetary wealth, power, and fame. Becoming a CEO of a large company, a movie star, or an elite athlete may bring great personal satisfaction, but unless ambition is paired with an altruistic attitude, it is unlikely to bring lasting contentment.

One of the best-regarded movies of all time, *Citizen Kane*, tells the rise and fall of an American tycoon who makes a fortune in the newspaper business but in the end dies a lonely and broken man who has never recovered from the lack of love in his childhood. On his deathbed, Kane's last word is "Rosebud," recalling the sled — bearing the image of a rosebud — with which he was happily playing when his newly wealthy parents told him they were sending him away to be properly educated. The sled stands for the comfort, love, and innocence of which he was deprived by his parents' ambitions for his career. Even the ruthless and successful Kane learns in the end that wealth means little if we don't experience love.

In searching for meaning, we may want to imagine ourselves at the end of life. What might we do that would make us think at the end, "This was a life worth living"? If we have made a positive difference in people's lives, if our families and friends have felt our love and care, their lives have been enriched and made happier because of us. We may die happily knowing that our love is leaving the world a little better than when we entered it.

A friend of mine used to work in a lung cancer unit at a hospital. She met many patients who had only weeks to live. When reflecting on their lives, almost all patients expressed regret at not spending more time with their loved ones. If there was one thing they would have done differently, it was to have spent less time working and more time with family and friends. It is always tragic when the recognition of the right choice comes too late. Fortunately, for most of us there is time to reconsider our priorities.

16. Mastering the Art of Love

It is easy to hate, and it is difficult to love. This is how the whole scheme of things works. All good things are difficult to achieve; and bad things are very easy to get. — CONFUCIUS

Can love be learned? In principle, yes, but there are several important requirements. Love necessitates a positive, embracing view of ourselves and of life. Fromm claimed that only a person who has reached developmental maturity is truly capable of loving. Such maturity implies self-acceptance and overcoming narcissism. Love requires humility. We are not truly concerned with the happiness and well-being of somebody else if we perceive ourselves as superior. Finally, love requires awareness and sensitivity to recognize the needs of the beloved for attaining well-being and happiness.

Like mastering any art, learning to love takes concentration, discipline, and patience. The principle of the art of love is actually quite easy: all we need to do is avoid egotistic impulses and remain focused on loving thoughts and activities. We should view ourselves not as separate from others but rather as part of humanity, a part of life.

In practice, maintaining a constant focus on love is exceedingly difficult. Try it for five minutes and see. For just five minutes, monitor the thoughts or impulses that arise in your mind. Try to keep your focus on somebody or something you love. What has your partner or child done today? Is there something you can do to make their day a little better? What do they like? Have you said something nice to them lately?

Whenever your thoughts stray away from your focus on loving, notice it. Did you think about the football game later today? The errands you have to run? Your job? Going out with friends? Assess whether your thoughts are self-serving or loving, that is, directed at the well-being and happiness of somebody else.

You will probably find that it is very hard to maintain this focus even for this short time. When we realize that mastering the art of loving requires maintaining a focus on love for every waking minute of our day, it becomes very clear what kind of challenge it is.

The practice of rejecting egotistic impulses in favor of loving is known to be effective for attaining happiness. Some devout followers of religions that teach similar precepts have achieved a state of deep contentment. In other words, if we manage to maintain control of our self-serving impulses and concentrate on love, we will achieve happiness. Guaranteed.

Think about this for a moment. There is a *proven, guaranteed* way to attain lasting happiness. Something anybody can achieve. No tricks. Why isn't everybody lining up for this? Because the process is hard. All major successes in life are earned the hard way.

We have a choice. At any given time, we can set our priorities. We can spend most of our lives focusing on our job to achieve what society defines as success, and maybe we will find some satisfaction. Maybe. Or we can spend our time developing our focus on love, and we will surely attain happiness. Seems like an easy choice. It also means that anybody truly wanting to achieve happiness can do so. We just have to put the effort into it.

Contentment results from the way our mind processes thoughts, actions, and events. The same event may elicit very different responses in people. For example, let's imagine two drivers getting rear-ended in their cars. One jumps out screaming in anger over his damaged property, while the other expresses gratitude that nobody got hurt. A missed putt on a golf course may appear to one person as a personal failure, while another laughs about it as bad luck. We can perceive the same events, and our whole lives, as wonderful or dreadful — it's our choice. If we want to perceive it as wonderful, however, we may need to work at it.

A critical component of loving is concentration. In loving, our mind is focused on the well-being and happiness of another person. This may be easy at times but difficult when our mind is flooded with competing demands. If I look at my wife with a focus on love, I actively look for ways to improve her day, to take responsibilities off her shoulders, and to make her feel loved. If I look at her without such a focus, my mind may be distracted by thoughts of my work, leisure activities, or something else. Maintaining a focus on love means we are concerned about the well-being and happiness of the beloved at all times, while carefully weighing our own needs.

Over the centuries, people have developed various techniques for maintaining a focus on love. The Buddha taught exercises in mindfulness and meditation to improve our focus on everything we do. These practices are effective and still popular today. They involve training the mind to live in every moment without constantly assessing it. The result is that we gain control over our impulses, conquer distractions, and allow love to flourish freely. Instead of thinking about our lives all the time, we *experience* life in every moment. Like learning to focus on love, however, mindfulness training is hard. Formal meditation, in particular, is not for everybody: it requires sitting still for an extended period each day. Many feel they cannot incorporate such a commitment into their daily lives. Nowadays, meditation teachers offer practices that fit more easily into people's schedules, such as brief periods of meditation with the aid of smartphone applications, or walking meditation.

Another proven method for mastering selflessness is

praying. Prayers in most religions involve focusing on love, usually love of God. Prayer serves the same essential purpose as mindfulness training, teaching us to control impulses, and it requires similar hard work to achieve results. Some may find that prayer has a motivational advantage over meditation without spiritual guidance: if we believe in the reward of heaven or a similarly appealing afterlife, we may be more inclined to follow through.

While practices like meditation and prayer improve our focus on love, they typically occupy only a small fraction of our days, leaving us exposed to self-serving drives for much of the time. How can we learn to be mindful of our thoughts and actions *all* the time? We may do this step by step, starting by spending a few minutes a day trying to achieve a dedicated focus. For example, each time we get into our car, we might dedicate fifteen minutes of driving time to total concentration on our driving — avoiding other thoughts. We might start with only ten or five minutes and extend the time as we make progress. We may use any downtime during the day, like waiting in line, for mind exercises, which improve our awareness of our thoughts. Some people like to set an alarm every hour to take one minute to focus on love. What we think about during these few minutes may vary, but in general, it involves asking ourselves how we can make life nicer for those around us. These exercises are essentially mindfulness training that is specifically applied to the art of loving.

Any glimpse of awareness of the constant influence of egotistic impulses is a step toward our goal, and we immediately feel its effect. As soon as we reject such an impulse, we feel contentment. To identify a self-serving drive, we just have to ask ourselves if a particular inclination is directed at helping ourselves or others. For example, thinking about going to the golf course is serving our drive for pleasure (unless we do it solely to please a friend who asked us to go along). While there is nothing wrong with enjoying a round of golf, we need to realize that the satisfaction is brief.

In contrast, spending time on loving activities, such as visiting our parents, taking the children out, and doing household tasks, is associated with lasting contentment because these activities increase the happiness of others. Obviously, some self-serving impulses are essential to follow, including eating, drinking, and sleeping. Taking time for ourselves for exercise, recuperation, and rest also is critical. We should strive, however, to remain mindful of love all the time.

The bad news is that there is no easy way to maintain our focus on love. Meditation, prayers, and mindfulness exercises typically require years of practice to master. Each of us has to figure out what method works best for us, but all approaches require discipline and patience. Whether and to what extent we succeed largely depends on how important the goal of mastering the art of love is to us. If we prioritize it over other concerns, we will make good progress. The good news is that it gets easier with practice.

Many will feel that the entire process sounds dreadful and antithetical to the ease and spontaneity we associate with love. Unfortunately, love is *not* magical in the sense that it simply comes over us and remains forever. Love *is* magical because it is life's amazing, central force.

Another way to think about this undertaking is as a wonderful opportunity to choose a certain path to happiness. Focusing on love requires work, but the dedication pays off. It's like learning to ride a bicycle: at first, it is hard and requires our full concentration. Once we have mastered the skill, we don't even have to think about it.

We tend to proceed along the path of least resistance. The lures of instant gratification are tempting. When we feel anger, it is gratifying to release it by swearing or acting out. When we feel aggression, it seems empowering to channel all that energy into acts of violence. When we feel lustful, it is rewarding to engage in sex. Giving in to these impulses is easy, but they bring only short-term satisfaction, and sometimes they endanger our chances of experiencing lasting love.

Self-serving impulses may actually have detrimental rather than self-preserving effects in the long run. When we follow our impulse to eat in excess and to watch TV instead of being physically active, we may put ourselves at risk of obesity, diabetes, high blood pressure, and heart disease. Egotism is shortsighted, whereas selfless love brings lasting rewards and benefits to the giver as well as the recipient.

One of the most significant advancements in human evolution is the ability to envision the long-term consequences of our actions. This capacity enables us to control our impulses for aggression or anger: we can weigh the short-term satisfaction they offer against the benefit of longer-term contentment that we derive from focusing on love.

Even with this rational ability, however, most of us find it challenging to control our impulses and do not always succeed. It is conceivable that we are in an evolutionary transition period, evolving from instinct-driven into instinct-controlled beings. Future generations may learn complete command over their impulses through training in childhood, which may result in a world of happy, loving people — nirvana for all.

Love is one of many innate impulses. However, our ability to love can be fully developed only if other competing impulses are controlled. Starting in childhood, when we first develop a sense of self (an important milestone in our cognitive growth), most individuals develop egocentric needs that demand satisfaction. While young children also show an inclination toward altruism, this capacity must be encouraged if it is to develop.[1]

To what extent the ability to love grows without parental guidance is unclear. Like most drives and impulses, this capacity varies from person to person. My son, Luca, has Down syndrome. It seems individuals with this genetic makeup tend to be less self-centered and more generous toward others — an observation that may suggest altruism is influenced by genetic factors.

Indeed, there is evidence from evolutionary biology for the existence of gene constellations associated with altruism.[2] Some people find it harder than others to control self-serving impulses. Some individuals, for example, are born with a very competitive drive, and they struggle to control their temper when things are not going their way. Others are more even-tempered and seem to intuitively gravitate toward suppressing their own interests for the benefit of others. As with most genetic predispositions, however, our innate impulses can be greatly modified by our own intervention and by our environment.

Karin is an administrative assistant at the hospital where I work. In the ten years I have known her, I have never seen her angry, moody, or anything less than cheerful. She always greets people with a smile and genuinely cares about them. If you are not doing well, she'll do her best to help you. She seems to have endless energy to help anyone in need. People who know her well say that's the way she has always been. Is Karin just this way because she was born with a heart of gold?

Karin says she wasn't. Like many of us, she used to be irritable and even lashed out at times. One day, she had a big fight with her daughter over some banality. They did not speak for weeks, and Karin even developed migraines as a result of the stress. Eventually, Karin recognized the absurdity of their actions and apologized to her daughter (even though they were both at fault). From that day on, Karin decided never to let her anger get control of her again. "Life's too short for such nonsense," she said, and she has been focusing on the positive aspects of life ever since. Confronted with the temptation to give in to frustration or sadness, she chooses love of life and people every time.

Environment can be critically important to developing our ability to love. Loving parents will reward any selfless action by a child, thereby associating selflessness with a pleasurable outcome and reinforcing loving behavior. Controlling self-directed impulses is a lifelong challenge. Consciously or not, we are constantly selecting among many impulses. Driving in heavy traffic, we may feel an impulse to cut in front of another car to get ahead. When our boss reprimands us for no good reason, we may feel aggression and anger.

Through education in childhood, conscious reflection, or experience, we learn that rejecting egotistic impulses is actually more rewarding than yielding to them. The wisdom said to come with age may be attributed in large part to having learned to curb egotism.

To master the art of loving, we must make it the most important thing in life. Love is a delicate flower that needs nurturing and protection to bloom. Lack of attention may easily lead to its demise.

No matter how hard we try, few of us will truly be able to master selfless love as figures like Jesus or the Buddha have done. For most of us, it is too hard to control self-serving impulses all the time and to love our neighbors, who may not themselves be loving. Why should we be nice to those who are inconsiderate toward us? Don't we also have the right to protect our own peace of mind?

Some may even argue that there are disadvantages to

being too loving. People may take advantage of us, walk all over us. In fact, some people probably will, and they may even consider us dumb or naive for allowing ourselves to be used. This prospect may seem intolerable. Masters in the art of loving, however, will say that those who take advantage of us bring misery on themselves: they will not achieve happiness. Maintaining a focus on love, on the other hand, keeps us happy. It's a function of our biology.

Still, many of us find it more practical to extend love only to those we deem worthy of it. We need to realize, though, that we indulge anger or resentment at the price of our own happiness. Animosity robs us of our own contentment. If we withhold love or love only selectively, we will never truly master the art of loving.

Of course, not everyone wants to become a master of love. We may feel we don't want to become saints, or that a constant struggle for selflessness will prevent us from having fun. Indeed, many feel that life's ups and downs are essential components in living — removing all pain and suffering may not be the critical goal to all. The good news is that we do not have to go to extremes. It's our choice. Nobody is forcing us to continue our training to the master level. We all can find the true "middle way" that suits us best.

We may want to remember, however, that every effort counts. Even if we take only a few minutes each day to remind ourselves of the importance of loving, we are one step further along the path. And those few minutes bring instant rewards. As soon as we put our priorities into perspective, we feel more content.

Leaving the house in the morning, we may be overwhelmed with thoughts of all the things we have to accomplish. But if we examine these obligations closely, those feelings of stress and pressure may subside. How critical are these tasks to our life? What will happen if we don't accomplish any of them? What are the truly important things in life? It becomes clear that few of the things we stress about are of critical importance. What matters is the happiness of those we love and the time we spend with them.

Every morning we can make an effort to think of love and say it out loud. Every day we can try to think of at least one loving thing to do. Whenever we have a quiet moment, we can bring love to mind. The effect on our outlook and those around us can be substantial.

Focusing on love and the happiness of others does not mean that we have to give up on our career or other goals: the key is to find a balance. We may navigate our lives more easily when we align our quest for love with societal norms and avoid alienating family or friends in our pursuit of perfection.

Careers may pose a particular challenge. The intention to be loving may directly conflict with the goal of professional advancement. In my profession of academic medicine, promotion is heavily dependent on publishing scientific papers. Most research studies involve a team of investigators, and the greatest credit for a publication goes to the author whose name appears first. Accordingly, researchers may compete fiercely and bitterly for the position of first author. It may be challenging to maintain our focus on love when we see colleagues acting in self-serving ways, claiming undeserved credit, and advancing professionally by doing so. It requires commitment to our goals and our training in the art of loving.

Ultimately, we control how much happiness we attain in life. Many people, while committed to nurturing love and restraining egotism, would also like to enjoy professional success and occasional self-indulgent pleasures and excitement. Such an approach to life may not lead to the highest possible level of contentment, but it may be a more realistic path.

Just as some people are more loving than others, there are also some people who seem easier to love, and some people may seem easier to love at some times than at others. No matter how much we may love our partner or our children, at times we may not feel much affection for them because we are distracted by another impulse, such as anger or frustration, or simply because we are focusing on something else. Such moments illustrate the importance of focus. Conscious attention to loving affects not only the love we give but also the love we actually feel.

The more negative attributes we associate with a person, the more difficult it is for us to focus on loving them: sometimes it may seem impossible. A master recognizes that negative attributes are a matter of perception. To Jesus, there were no bad people, and thus he loved all.

A father who refuses to extend his love to his daughter because she is gay ascribes a negative attribute to her that is of his own creation. Another father in the same situation sees the goodness and beauty in his daughter and embraces her individuality. Loving depends entirely on our state of mind. We may find it much easier to love our partner and children than to extend our love to others, but — with focus — we can develop affection for all.

17. A Call for Teaching Love

A great irony of human existence is that love, which is arguably the single most desired goal in life, is so poorly understood and so hard for us to master. Given its importance, we might expect that enormous resources would be spent on understanding how to attain love. For many human endeavors, there is extensive literature explaining how to achieve mastery and institutions that specialize in understanding and teaching those skills. For love, there is no preparation or formal training. We are expected to learn from our families and by experience.

The fading influence of religion and the growing commercialization of love may increasingly confuse us in our quest for a happy and fulfilled life. The strong focus on academic and financial success in Western societies has led to a neglect of personal growth. This is a particularly acute problem for adolescents and young adults. Annual polls report that 45 percent of high school students felt "major" academic pressure in 2008, up from

19 percent in 2001.[1] In a 2013 survey by the American Psychological Association, teenagers reported stress levels that equaled or even exceeded those perceived by adults, with approximately one-third of teens exhibiting signs of depression.[2] To cope with increased stress, teenagers turn more frequently to alcohol and drugs.[3] Most sadly, suicide rates increased by almost one-quarter (!) between 1999 and 2014 in the United States, with the greatest increase among females seen in girls aged ten to fourteen.[4]

As a society, we must reconsider our priorities and our obligations to our children. While the exact causes of the increase in depression and suicide rates are uncertain, it is intuitive that increasing pressure in school, societal expectations for physical attractiveness, economic concerns, and weaker emotional support structures are important factors.

Children learn skills and knowledge in school to prepare them to achieve what we define as success in life: history, sciences, mathematics, and languages. However, we are well aware that they will forget much of this information within a few years. We also school our children to become "productive" members of our society, conforming to social norms for occupation and income. More than anything, however, our children would benefit from an education in love and personal development to prepare them for life.

We may see this task as the parents' job, but how can parents teach it if they themselves struggle to understand love? We may see teaching love as a function of religious institutions, but religious education may come with constraints on a child's independent thinking. In any case, religious training for children and adolescents is rapidly waning. In 2014, the Pew Research Center found that 35 percent of young adults (aged 18–29) in the United States had no religious affiliation.[5]

Yet the teen years are a notoriously vulnerable period for children. Hormonal changes increase susceptibility to depression, contributing to teenagers' feeling of isolation.[6] At a time when children may feel not well understood by their parents, they might benefit from guidance on dealing with emotions and relationships. More than one hundred research studies have found a positive effect of religion or spirituality on adolescents' mental health.[7] Given the waning of religion in our society, there is an increasing void of emotional support for teenagers, leaving them vulnerable to anxiety, depression, and substance abuse. This void could be filled with education about love.

Education in the basic principles of love could help children and adolescents develop a more mature picture of love and avoid mistakes that may have long-term consequences, such as unwanted pregnancies, sexually transmitted diseases, or unhealthy relationships. Importantly, learning about love would complement their physical and intellectual development, giving them confidence to deal with societal pressures and associated stress. Teaching our youth the fundamental principles of love would allow them to reflect on the nature of human existence, providing them essential guidance for their development.

Children who recognize the critical need to love themselves and also accept love — without the need for external validation — are better positioned to face life. Fostering children's belief in their individuality and value may help them accept themselves for who they are, which may help them resist negative societal pressures and expectations. By teaching children that each person's value arises from being a unique individual with a capability to love, we could help them understand that academic achievement and appearance are irrelevant to a person's worth. This realization could help children to enjoy their childhoods and find balance in their later lives.

Growing into a loving person takes devotion, knowledge, and maturity, and it is a process that extends well beyond childhood. We can, however, lay the foundation in every child to find love and mature into a loving person. We can teach children that love starts with awareness of our actions and thoughts; that love is innate in all of us, but we must protect it against competing, self-serving impulses; that love is not a stroke of fortune but something that is under their own control; that anyone can attain love if they devote effort and focus to it. This may be the single most important realization that we can give to our children. It gives them power to shape their lives.

Practically speaking, how could we educate children in love? We might consider initiating classes about the art of loving in seventh or eighth grade, with discussions of the philosophy of love and the teachings of thinkers, like Socrates, Confucius, and others. Classes could continue throughout high school, ending with contemporary thinking and discussions on love. The key objectives for these classes would be to recognize the obsessive aspects of falling in love; the difference between infatuation and mature, lasting love, as well as between lust and love; and the principle that love can be learned by redirecting our mind's focus from selfishness to genuine care for others. Classes might also explore the interconnection of human drives and their effect on our mental and emotional states. High school and college classes could explore the philosophical, spiritual, biological, and psychological aspects of love in greater depth. All classes should give credit for attendance only and not burden students with additional academic assignments and pressure.

Our education system, whose basic structure dates from the nineteenth century, has not kept up with the demands of today's world or a rapidly changing society.[8] Unfortunately, it will take many years to reform our education system to any significant degree. In the meantime, the fundamentals of love might be taught in health studies classes, along with topics in biology and sexuality. But a better option would be an entirely new curriculum focusing on personal development.

As a society, we should decide what is truly relevant for the education of our children. Given the evidence of increasing stress, depression, and suicide rates among teenagers, it is time to pause and rethink our priorities. Among these priorities must be to allow our children to explore their enormous capacity for love.

Conclusion

We all have hopes, dreams, and desires that inspire our lives. Ultimately, we have to find purpose in our existence as well as comfort with who we are and where we are going. We all strive to attain happiness in life.

If we agree on this common goal, we may ask ourselves how we can reliably achieve it. We recognize that love is a key factor in realizing happiness, yet we are drawn toward all kinds of endeavors in life *except* a systematic exploration of the nature of love. Some regard love as inherently elusive.

From a pragmatic point of view, attempting to understand love and the mechanisms leading to happiness is likely to increase our chance of success. Any attempt to understand a phenomenon must start with defining or at least describing it. In the English language, the word *love* has different meanings depending on the context, adding to the confusion in our ideas of love. In the context of relationships, a unifying concept of love emerges once we identify and distinguish other emotions that we associate with love.

Central to this concept is the distinction between love and relationships. The common denominator of romantic and nonromantic love is the *urge and continuous effort for the happiness and well-being of somebody.* In contrast to nonromantic relationships, we may experience passion and sexual attraction with romantic bonds, but the force we identify as love is the same in both types of relationship. Not only does neuroscience support this concept, but it also helps us understand the dynamics of romantic and nonromantic relationships, including the confusion about love's selfless character. Love itself — as the phenomenon — is always selfless, while relationships commonly require reciprocity.

To understand how love is implicated in the perception of happiness, we need to appreciate our physiology and the context in which love develops. Love is one of many drives that motivate our actions and thoughts. Because of its significance for ourselves and our species, focusing on love brings lasting neurochemical and emotional rewards, whereas other drives are linked only to short-term satisfaction, often followed by remorse. Yet many of these other drives are powerful, and we perpetually seek their gratification.

Unlike animals, human beings are able to consciously choose among the drives we want to follow. Thus, we are in control of our love and happiness: they are indeed choices. Unfortunately, to attain such control is difficult because most of us are unaware of our drives and their influence on our mind. Furthermore, because we typically assert little control of our impulses while growing up, it can be difficult to learn how to do it later in life. Ideally, we should help our children develop awareness and control over their drives — that is, teach them the art of love — at a young age.

Disentangling love from religion is a challenging task. Is religion preoccupied with love because love is divine or because it values love as an essential force of human existence (but does not recognize its biological nature)? Both views can be supported, and, of course, biology itself can also be viewed as divine or God-given. Theists and atheists alike may benefit from focusing on the practice of love rather than arguing for the correctness of their hypotheses. While love cannot explain the purpose of all life, it can provide guidance for purposeful living. With or without the structure of religion, love provides answers for a happy, fulfilled life.

Lack of love damages not only personal relationships but all human interactions, particularly at the level of societal and world affairs. Almost everyone wants to live happily and peacefully. Those who are antagonistic toward others — reflecting their ignorance of our biological imperatives — harm not only those around them but also themselves. It is our confusion over the many impulses we experience that prevents us from enjoying greater unity.

We all face choices among the many drives acting upon us every minute of our lives — most of which we are unaware of. In our quest for happiness in life, we steer our ship through all weather, alongside sirens and sea monsters. The journey is not a sheer pleasure cruise for any of us. Sometimes the sea is calm, and we can enjoy a beautiful ride. Other times we have to find our way through darkness and storms. Many great thinkers and spiritual leaders have built lighthouses along our way, and their beams illuminate one course: be wary of temptations to serve ourselves, and follow the light of love.

Acknowledgments

As with any discussion on theoretical concepts, proof of validity exists in the plausibility of the argument and in its confirmation by others. I am indebted to the many colleagues, scholars, and other individuals who engaged in personal and online discussions of the concepts presented in this book. I am especially grateful to the following individuals for their analyses and constructive critiques: Annemarie Boyan, Dominik Wild, and Ariane Wohlfarth. I am thankful to my publisher, New World Library, for trusting in the merit of this endeavor. My heartfelt gratitude also goes to my agent, Stephany Evans, and my editor, Georgia Hughes, for their considerate reviews and valuable suggestions to enhance the manuscript. My special thanks go to Erika Büky for her excellent manuscript editing and her many thoughtful and constructive comments.

My parents laid the foundation of love in me, for which I will always be thankful. My mother's eternal, indefatigable, and selfless care for my brother, Kian, and me will continue to serve as my ideal of parental love. I thank our own children, Ryan, Eric, Luca, and Zoe, not only for spurring my ambition to see this project through but also for providing me with perfect study models of love. Above all, my deepest appreciation and gratitude go to my beloved wife, Denise, who has been my most brilliant sounding board, my tireless emotional support, and the greatest inspiration for love I could ever imagine.

Notes

Introduction

1. E. Fromm, *The Art of Loving* (New York: Harper, 1956).
2. "Newly Discovered 1964 MLK Speech on Civil Rights, Segregation and Apartheid in South Africa," video and transcript, Democracy Now, www.democracynow.org/2016/1/18/newly_discovered_1964_mlk _speech_on, accessed September 18, 2016.

Chapter 1. What Is Love?

1. Fromm, *The Art of Loving*.
2. S. Zeki, "The Neurobiology of Love," *FEBS Lett* 581 (2007): 25–79; L. Starka, "Endocrine Factors of Pair Bonding," *Prague Med Rep* 108 (2007): 297–305; D. Marazziti and D. Canale, "Hormonal Changes When Falling in Love," *Psychoneuroendocrinology* 29 (2004): 931–36; E. Emanuele, P. Politi, M. Bianchi, P. Minoretti, M. Bertona, and D. Geroldi, "Raised Plasma Nerve Growth Factor Levels Associated with Early-Stage Romantic Love," *Psychoneuroendocrinology* 31 (2006): 288–94.
3. A. Bartels and S. Zeki, "The Neural Basis of Romantic Love," *Neuroreport* 11 (2000): 3829–34.
4. S. Ortigue, F. Bianchi-Demicheli, N. Patel, C. Frum, and J. W. Lewis, "Neuroimaging of Love: fMRI Meta-analysis Evidence toward New Perspectives in Sexual Medicine," *J Sex Med* 7 (2010): 3541–52.

5. H. E. Fisher, *Anatomy of Love: The Natural History of Monogamy, Adultery, and Divorce* (London: Simon & Schuster, 1992).

6. Ortigue et al., "Neuroimaging of Love."

7. Fisher, *Anatomy of Love.*

8. G. W. Leibniz, *The Shorter Leibniz Texts: A Collection of New Translations*, trans. Lloyd Strickland (London: Bloomsbury Academic, 2006), 189.

9. Zeki, "The Neurobiology of Love."

10. A. J. Hawkins and A. Tamara, "How Common Is Divorce and What Are the Reasons?," *Utah Divorce Orientation*, Utah State University Extension online course, www.divorce.usu.edu/lessons/lesson3, accessed June 13, 2017.

Chapter 2. Why Do We Love?

1. S. A. Kapadia, ed., *The Teachings of Zoroaster and the Philosophy of the Parsi Religion* (London: John Murray, 1905).

2. Plato, *The Symposium*, ed. W. Hamilton (London: Penguin Books, 1951).

3. C. S. Lewis, *The Four Loves* (London: Geoffrey Bles, 1960).

4. W. Schmidt-Biggemann, *Baruch de Spinoza, 1677–1977: His Work and Its Reception* (Baarn: Menno Hertzberger, 1977).

5. Arthur Schopenhauer, *The World as Will and Representation* (Indian Hills, CO: Falcon's Wing Press, 1958).

6. D. Loye, *Darwin in Love: The Rest of the Story* (Pacific Grove, CA: Osanto University Press, 2013).

7. S. Freud, S. Katz, and J. Riviere, *Freud: On War, Sex, and Neurosis* (New York: Arts & Science Press, 1947).

8. J. A. Lee, *Colours of Love: An Exploration of the Ways of Loving* (Toronto: New Press, 1973).

9. Robert J. Sternberg, *The Triangle of Love: Intimacy, Passion, Commitment* (New York: Basic Books, 1988).

10. B. P. Acevedo, A. Aron, H. E. Fisher, and L. L. Brown, "Neural Correlates of Long-Term, Intense Romantic Love," *Soc Cogn Affect Neurosci* 7 (2012): 145–59.

11. J. K. Kiecolt-Glaser, C. Bane, R. Glaser, and W. B. Malarkey, "Love, Marriage, and Divorce: Newlyweds' Stress Hormones Foreshadow Relationship Changes," *J Consult Clin Psychol* 71 (2003): 176–88.

12. Acevedo et al., "Neural Correlates of Long-Term, Intense Romantic Love."

13. Bartels and Zeki, "The Neural Basis of Romantic Love."

14. C. R. von Rueden and A. V. Jaeggi, "Men's Status and Reproductive Success in 33 Nonindustrial Societies: Effects of Subsistence, Marriage System, and Reproductive Strategy," *Proc Natl Acad Sci USA* 113, no. 39 (2016): 10824–29.

15. Loye, *Darwin in Love.*

16. H. E. Fisher, "The Drive to Love," in *The New Psychology of Love: The Neural Mechanism for Mate Selection*, ed. R. J. Sternberg and K. Weis (New Haven, CT: Yale University Press, 2006), 87–110.

17. E. Sober and D. S. Wilson, *Unto Others: The Evolution and Psychology of Unselfish Behavior* (Cambridge, MA: Harvard University Press, 1998).

18. T. F. Robles, R. B. Slatcher, J. M. Trombello, and M. M. McGinn, "Marital Quality and Health: A Meta-analytic Review," *Psychol Bull* 140 (2014): 140–87.

19. E. Fernandez-Duque and M. Huck, "Till Death (or an Intruder) Do Us Part: Intrasexual Competition in a Monogamous Primate," *PLoS One* 8 (2013): e53724.

20. Zeki, "The Neurobiology of Love."

21. H. E. Hershfield, C. Mogilner, and U. Barnea, "People Who Choose Time over Money Are Happier," *Soc Psych Personal Sci* 7 (2016): 697–706.

Chapter 3. Love as an Art

1. M. Soat, "Social Media Triggers Dopamine High," https://www.ama.org/publications/MarketingNews/Pages/feeding-the-addiction.aspx, accessed May 1, 2017.

2. D. I. Tamir and J. P. Mitchell, "Disclosing Information about the Self Is Intrinsically Rewarding," *Proc Natl Acad Sci USA* 109 (2012): 8038–43.

Chapter 4. Self-Love

1. A. C. Pegis, *Basic Writings of Saint Thomas Aquinas* (New York: Random House, 1945).

2. S. D. Lamborn, N. S. Mounts, L. Steinberg, and S. M. Dornbusch, "Patterns of Competence and Adjustment among Adolescents from Authoritative, Authoritarian, Indulgent, and Neglectful Families," *Child Dev* 62 (1991): 1049–65.

3. C. P. Niemiec, R. M. Ryan, and E. L. Deci, "The Path Taken: Consequences

of Attaining Intrinsic and Extrinsic Aspirations in Post-College Life,"
J Res Pers 73 (2009): 291–306.

4. M. E. Bernard, *Strength of Self-Acceptance: Theory, Practice, and Research* (New York: Springer, 2013).

Chapter 5. Love and Romantic Relationships

1. P. L. Reno, R. S. Meindl, M. A. McCollum, and C. O. Lovejoy, "Sexual Dimorphism in Australopithecus Afarensis Was Similar to That of Modern Humans," *Proc Natl Acad Sci USA* 100 (2003): 9404–9.

2. M. K. Zeitzen, *Polygamy: A Cross-Cultural Analysis* (New York: Berg, 2008).

3. K. D. O'Leary, B. P. Acevedo, A. Aron, H. Huddy, and D. Mashek, "Is Long-Term Love More Than a Rare Phenomenon? If So, What Are Its Correlates?," *Soc Psychol Personal Sci* 3 (2012): 241–49; B. P. Acevedo and A. Aron, "Does a Long-Term Relationship Kill Romantic Love?," *Rev Gen Psychol* 13 (2009): 59–65; A. Brewis and M. Meyer, "Marital Coitus across the Life Course," *J Biosoc Sci* 37 (2005): 499–518.

4. Brewis and Meyer, "Marital Coitus across the Life Course."

5. C. Liu, "Does Quality of Marital Sex Decline with Duration?," *Arch Sex Behav* 32 (2003): 55–60.

6. R. D. Conger, K. J. Conger, and M. J. Martin, "Socioeconomic Status, Family Processes, and Individual Development," *J Marriage Fam* 72 (2010): 685–704.

7. D. M. Rhule-Louie and R. J. McMahon, "Problem Behavior and Romantic Relationships: Assortative Mating, Behavior Contagion, and Desistance," *Clin Child Fam Psychol Rev* 10 (2007): 53–100.

8. D. M. Frost and C. Forrester, "Closeness Discrepancies in Romantic Relationships: Implications for Relational Well-Being, Stability, and Mental Health," *Pers Soc Psychol Bull* 39 (2013): 456–69.

9. Gary D. Chapman, *The Five Love Languages: How to Express Heartfelt Commitment to Your Mate* (Chicago: Northfield, 1995).

Chapter 6. Love and Sex

1. Freud, Katz, and Riviere, *Freud: On War, Sex, and Neurosis.*

2. H. E. Fisher, A. Aron, and L. L. Brown, "Romantic Love: A Mammalian Brain System for Mate Choice," *Philos Trans R Soc Lond B Biol Sci* 361 (2006): 2173–86.

3. Brewis and Meyer, "Marital Coitus across the Life Course."

4. A. J. Blow and K. Hartnett, "Infidelity in Committed Relationships, II: A Substantive Review," *J Marital Fam Ther* 31 (2005): 217–33.

5. V. Morell, "A New Look at Monogamy," *Science* 281 (1998): 1982–83.

6. J. Treas and D. Giesen, "Sexual Infidelity among Married and Cohabiting Americans," *J Marital Fam Ther* 62 (2000): 48–60.

Chapter 7. Love and Gender

1. J. Hutchison and D. Martin, "The Evolution of Stereotypes," in *Evolutionary Perspectives on Social Psychology*, ed. V. Zeigler-Hill , L. Welling, and T. Shackelford (Springer, 2015, ebook).

2. Sachverständigenrat deutscher Stiftungen für Integration und Migration, *Diskriminierung am Ausbildungsmarkt: Ausmaß, Ursachen und Handlungsperspektiven*, March 2014, www.svr-migration.de/publikationen /diskriminierung-am-ausbildungsmarkt, accessed August 4, 2017.

3. M. Ingalhalikar, A. Smith, D. Parker, T. D. Satterthwaite, M. A. Elliott, J. Ruparel, H. Hakonarson, R. E. Gur , R. C. Gur, and R. Verma, "Sex Differences in the Structural Connectome of the Human Brain," *Proc Natl Acad Sci USA* 111 (2014): 823–28.

4. D. Joel, Z. Berman, I. Tavor, N. Wexler, O. Gaber, Y. Stein, N. Shefi, et al., "Sex beyond the Genitalia: The Human Brain Mosaic," *Proc Natl Acad Sci USA* 112 (2015): 15468–73.

5. J. C. Chrisler and D. R. McCreary, eds., *Handbook of Gender Research in Psychology* (New York: Springer, 2010).

6. J. Gray, *Men Are from Mars, Women Are from Venus: A Practical Guide for Improving Communication and Getting What You Want in Your Relationships* (New York: HarperCollins, 1992).

7. R. F. Baumeister, K. R. Catanese, and K. D. Vohs, "Is There a Gender Difference in Strength of Sex Drive? Theoretical Views, Conceptual Distinctions, and a Review of Relevant Evidence," *Pers Soc Psychol Rev* 5 (2001): 242–73.

8. B. J. Carothers and H. T. Reis, "Men and Women Are from Earth: Examining the Latent Structure of Gender," *J Pers Soc Psychol* 104 (2013): 385–407.

Chapter 8. Love for Our Children

1. K. M. Kendrick, "The Neurobiology of Social Bonds," *J Neuroendocrinol* 16 (2004): 1007–8.

2. Quoted in L. Amir, "Plato's Theory of Love: Rationality as Passion," *Practical Philosophy* 4, no. 3 (2001): 6–14.

3. J. E. Swain, P. Kim, J. Spicer, S. S. Ho, C. J. Dayton, A. Elmadih, and K. M. Abel, "Approaching the Biology of Human Parental Attachment: Brain Imaging, Oxytocin and Coordinated Assessments of Mothers and Fathers," *Brain Res* 1580 (2014): 78–101.

4. Bertrand Russell, *The Conquest of Happiness* (New York: Liveright, 1930).

5. M. D. Ainsworth, "Attachments beyond Infancy," *Am Psychol* 44 (1989): 709–16.

6. N. L. Segal, "A Tale of Two Sisters," *Psychology Today*, November 3, 2015, www.psychologytoday.com/articles/201511/tale-two-sisters.

7. Khalil Gibran, *The Prophet* (New York: Alfred A. Knopf, 1923), 17.

8. T. J. Bouchard Jr., D. T. Lykken, M. McGue, N. L. Segal, and A. Tellegen, "Sources of Human Psychological Differences: The Minnesota Study of Twins Reared Apart," *Science* 250 (1990): 223–28.

9. N. G. Waller and P. R. Shaver, "The Importance of Nongenetic Influences on Romantic Love Styles: A Twin-Family Study," *Psychol Sci* 5 (1994): 268–74.

10. W. T. Dalton III, D. Frick-Horbury, and K. M. Kitzmann, "Young Adults' Retrospective Reports of Parenting by Mothers and Fathers: Associations with Current Relationship Quality," *J Gen Psychol* 133 (2006): 5–18.

Chapter 9. Love and Religion

1. T. W. R. Davids, *Buddhist Suttas* (Oxford: Clarendon Press, 1881).

2. Huston Smith, *The World's Religions: Our Great Wisdom Traditions* (San Francisco: HarperSanFrancisco, 1991).

3. WIN-Gallup International, *Global Index of Religiosity and Atheism*, July 2012, www.wingia.com/web/files/news/14/file/14.pdf, accessed July 28, 2017.

Chapter 10. Love and Society

1. S. Gerhardt, *The Selfish Society: How We All Forgot to Love One Another and Made Money Instead* (London: Simon & Schuster, 2010).

2. T. Reichert, "Sex in Advertising Research: A Review of Content, Effects, and Functions of Sexual Information in Consumer Advertising," *Annu Rev Sex Res* 13 (2002): 241–73.

Chapter 11. Love and the World

1. Friedrich W. Nietzsche, *Thus Spoke Zarathustra: A Book for All and None*, trans. T. Common (Edinburgh: T. N. Foulis, 1909).
2. Von Rueden and Jaeggi, "Men's Status and Reproductive Success."
3. C. G. Jung, *Über die Psychologie des Unbewussten* (Zurich: Rascher, 1943), 91.
4. L. Fenstermacher, L. Kuznar, T. Rieger, A. Speckhard, et al., *Protecting the Homeland from International and Domestic Terrorism Threats*, Topical Strategic Multi-layer Assessment (SMA) Multi-agency and Air Force Research Laboratory Multi-Disciplinary White Papers in Support of Counterterrorism and Counter-WMD, January 2010, www.start.umd .edu/sites/default/files/files/publications/U_Counter_Terrorism _White_Paper_Final_January_2010.pdf, accessed July 28, 2017.
5. L. C. Gardner and M. B. Young, *Iraq and the Lessons of Vietnam, or How Not to Learn from the Past* (New York: New Press, 2007).
6. G. P. Shultz, "A Changed World: A Lecture Delivered at the Library of Congress on February 11, 2004" (Washington, DC: Library of Congress, 2004).
7. S. Bok, *A Strategy for Peace: Human Values and the Threat of War* (New York: Pantheon Books, 1989).
8. G. F. Kennan, *The Decline of Bismarck's European Order: Franco-Russian Relations, 1875–1890* (Princeton, NJ: Princeton University Press, 1981).
9. Richard M. Langworth, *Churchill and the Avoidable War: Could World War II Have Been Prevented?* (CreateSpace Independent Publishing Platform, 2015, ebook).

Chapter 12. Love and Human Differences

1. H. Tajfel, *Social Identity and Intergroup Relations* (Cambridge: Cambridge University Press, 1982).
2. Diogenes Laertius, *The Lives and Opinions of Eminent Philosophers*, trans. C. D. Yonge (London: H. G. Bohn, 1853).
3. Katherine W. Phillips, "How Diversity Makes Us Smarter," *Scientific American*, October 1, 2014, www.scientificamerican.com/article/how -diversity-makes-us-smarter/.
4. B. Piel, "Lüchow schafft das," *Spiegel Online*, October 13, 2015, www.spiegel.de/panorama/luechow-im-wendland-wie-eine-kleinstadt -die-fluechtlingskrise-meistert-a-1057348.html.

5. Heather Horn, "Where Does Fear of Refugees Come From?," *The Atlantic*, April 27, 2016, www.theatlantic.com/international/archive /2016/04/refugees-crime-rumors/480171/.

6. S. Lyons-Padilla, M. J. Gelfand, H. Mirahmadi, M. Farooq, and M. van Egmond, "Belonging Nowhere: Marginalization and Radicalization Risk among Muslim Immigrants," *Behavioral Science and Policy* 1, no. 2 (2015).

Chapter 13. Love and Happiness

1. Daniel Gilbert, *Stumbling on Happiness* (New York: Knopf, 2006).

2. A. Okbay, B. M. Baselmans, J. E. De Neve, P. Turley, M. G. Nivard, M. A. Fontana, S. F. Meddens, et al., "Genetic Variants Associated with Subjective Well-Being, Depressive Symptoms, and Neuroticism Identified through Genome-Wide Analyses," *Nat Genet* 48 (2016): 624–33.

3. Russell, *The Conquest of Happiness*.

4. R. F. C. Hull, ed., *C. G. Jung Speaking: Encounters and Interviews* (Princeton, NJ: Princeton University Press, 1987), 450–51.

Chapter 14. Love and Health

1. T. F. Robles and J. K. Kiecolt-Glaser, "The Physiology of Marriage: Pathways to Health," *Physiol Behav* 79 (2003): 409–16.

2. J. Holt-Lunstad, T. B. Smith, and J. B. Layton, "Social Relationships and Mortality Risk: A Meta-analytic Review," *PLoS Med* 7 (2010): e1000316.

3. T. F. Robles, R. B. Slatcher, J. M. Trombello, and M. M. McGinn, "Marital Quality and Health: A Meta-analytic Review," *Psychol Bull* 140 (2014): 140–87.

4. T. Buckley, S. Y. Hoo, J. Fethney, E. Shaw, P. S. Hanson, and G. H. Tofler, "Triggering of Acute Coronary Occlusion by Episodes of Anger," *Eur Heart J Acute Cardiovasc Care* 4 (2015): 493–98.

5. S. W. Cole, J. P. Capitanio, K. Chun, J. M. Arevalo, J. Ma, and J. T. Cacioppo, "Myeloid Differentiation Architecture of Leukocyte Transcriptome Dynamics in Perceived Social Isolation," *Proc Natl Acad Sci USA* 112 (2015): 15142–47.

6. I. S. Wittstein, D. R. Thiemann, J. A. Lima, K. L. Baughman, S. P. Schulman, G. Gerstenblith, K. C. Wu, J. J. Rade, T. J. Bivalacqua, and H. C. Champion, "Neurohumoral Features of Myocardial Stunning due to Sudden Emotional Stress," *N Engl J Med* 352 (2005): 539–48.

7. B. Ditzen and M. Heinrichs, "Psychobiology of Social Support: The

Social Dimension of Stress Buffering," *Restor Neurol Neurosci* 32 (2014): 149–62.

8. J. J. Legros, "Inhibitory Effect of Oxytocin on Corticotrope Function in Humans: Are Vasopressin and Oxytocin Yin-Yang Neurohormones?" *Psychoneuroendocrinology* 26 (2001): 649–55.

9. S. G. Post, "Altruism, Happiness, and Health: It's Good to Be Good," *Int J Behav Med* 12 (2005): 66–77.

Chapter 15. Love and the Meaning of Life

1. T. Devine, J. H. Seuk, and A. Wilson, *Cultivating Heart and Character: Educating for Life's Most Essential Goals* (Chapel Hill, NC: Character Development Pub., 2000); Virtue in Action, *Happiness: What Fortune and Fame Can't Buy*, April 2007, www.virtueinaction.com/2007/VIA _Happiness.pdf.

2. E. Sullivan, J. Annest, F. Luo, T. Simon, and L. Dahlberg, "Suicide among Adults Aged 35–64 Years: United States, 1999–2010," *MMWR* 62: (2013): 321–25.

Chapter 16. Mastering the Art of Love

1. F. Warneken and M. Tomasello, "Varieties of Altruism in Children and Chimpanzees," *Trends Cogn Sci* 13 (2009): 397–402.

2. G. J. Thompson, P. L. Hurd, and B. J. Crespi, "Genes Underlying Altruism," *Biol Lett* 9, no. 6 (2013): 20130395.

Chapter 17. A Call for Teaching Love

1. S. J. Cech, "Academic Pressure on Rise for Teens, Poll Finds," *Education Week*, August 5, 2008, www.edweek.org/ew/articles/2008/08/05 /45youth_web.h27.html.

2. American Psychological Association, *Stress in America: Are Teens Adopting Adults' Stress Habits?*, February 11, 2014, www.apa.org/news /press/releases/stress/2013/stress-report.pdf.

3. N. R. Leonard, M. V. Gwadz, A. Ritchie, J. L. Linick, C. M. Cleland, L. Elliott, and M. Grethel, "A Multi-method Exploratory Study of Stress, Coping, and Substance Use among High School Youth in Private Schools," *Front Psychol* 6 (2015): 1028.

4. Sally C. Curtin, Margaret Warner, and Holly Hedegaard, *Increase in Suicide in the United States, 1999–2014*, Centers for Disease Control and

Prevention, National Center for Health Statistics, NCHS Data Brief No. 241, April 2016.

5. Pew Research Center, *Religious Landscape Study*, www.pewforum.org /religious-landscape-study, accessed October 1, 2016.

6. E. J. Susman, L. D. Dorn, and G. P. Chrousos, "Negative Affect and Hormone Levels in Young Adolescents: Concurrent and Predictive Perspectives," *J Youth Adolesc* 20 (1991): 167–90.

7. R. E. Dew, S. S. Daniel, T. D. Armstrong, D. B. Goldston, M. F. Triplett, and H. G. Koenig, "Religion/Spirituality and Adolescent Psychiatric Symptoms: A Review," *Child Psychiatry Hum Dev* 39 (2008): 381–98.

8. T. Wagner and T. Dintersmith, *Most Likely to Succeed: How to Prepare Our Kids for the Innovation Era* (New York: Scribner, 2015).

Index

Page references followed by *fig* indicate an illustration.

About the Author

Armin A. Zadeh, MD, PhD, MPH, is a professor at Johns Hopkins University. He has authored more than one hundred scientific articles and is an editor of scholarly books in medicine. He is a regular speaker at national and international scientific meetings and directs educational events around the world.

As a cardiologist and scientist, Dr. Zadeh knows firsthand the close relationship between heart disease and state of mind. The loss of love can literally cause a broken heart — a form of severe heart disease. Drawing from his clinical and research experience, Dr. Zadeh has used his skills in the analysis and synthesis of complex data to formulate new concepts and hypotheses on love and happiness and to develop a framework to understand — and master — love, tested by a wide online readership. This framework integrates contemplations from philosophy and religion with insights into human biology.

Dr. Zadeh was born and educated in Düsseldorf, Germany, where he attended medical school. After initial postgraduate training in Germany and the United Kingdom, he came to the United States in 1995 to complete his education and training in medicine, public health, and research. He is married and lives with his family in the United States.

NEW WORLD LIBRARY is dedicated to publishing books and other media that inspire and challenge us to improve the quality of our lives and the world.

We are a socially and environmentally aware company. We recognize that we have an ethical responsibility to our customers, our staff members, and our planet.

We serve our customers by creating the finest publications possible on personal growth, creativity, spirituality, wellness, and other areas of emerging importance. We serve New World Library employees with generous benefits, significant profit sharing, and constant encouragement to pursue their most expansive dreams.

As a member of the Green Press Initiative, we print an increasing number of books with soy-based ink on 100 percent postconsumer-waste recycled paper. Also, we power our offices with solar energy and contribute to non-profit organizations working to make the world a better place for us all.

Our products are available in bookstores everywhere.

www.newworldlibrary.com

At NewWorldLibrary.com you can download our catalog,
subscribe to our e-newsletter, read our blog,
and link to authors' websites, videos, and podcasts.

Find us on Facebook, follow us on Twitter, and watch us on YouTube.

Send your questions and comments our way!
You make it possible for us to do what we love to do.

Phone: 415-884-2100 or 800-972-6657
Catalog requests: Ext. 10 | Orders: Ext. 10 | Fax: 415-884-2199
escort@newworldlibrary.com

NEW WORLD LIBRARY
publishing books that change lives   14 Pamaron Way, Novato, CA 94949